Brunches
lunches & treats

THE AUSTRALIAN
Women's Weekly

British and North American readers:
Please note that Australian cup and spoon measurements are metric.
A quick conversion guide appears on page 119.

contents

We're a sociable lot – whether it's a backyard barbie or a swish dinner party, we love getting together with friends to have a good time *and* a good meal. And why not? Sharing food and laughs with your nearest and dearest has just *got* to be good for what ails you! And, since this book's intention is to make *Brunches, lunches & treats* quick and easy as well as to suggest delicious-sounding menus, you'll find that, even as the cook, you'll be able to sit back, relax and enjoy the meal too.

Pamela Clark

Food Director

late breakfasts

grilled figs

with ricotta and honeycomb on toasted fruit bread

preparation time 5 minutes
cooking time 10 minutes

Honeycomb is the structure made of beeswax that houses the honey; this edible chewy comb, saturated with honey, is available in health food stores and some supermarkets.

8 large fresh figs, halved (approximately 650g)
1 tablespoon brown sugar
500g loaf fruit bread
2 cups (400g) ricotta cheese
150g honeycomb, sliced thickly
2 tablespoons honey

1 Place figs, cut-side up, on oven tray; sprinkle with sugar. Cook under hot grill about 5 minutes or until sugar melts and figs are browned lightly.

2 Cut bread into 1cm slices; toast both sides under hot grill.

3 Divide toast among serving plates; top each serving with equal amounts of ricotta and honeycomb, then top with two fig halves and drizzle with honey.

SERVES 8

per serving 6.8g fat; 1118kJ

tip Walnut or almond bread can be substituted for the fruit loaf, if you prefer.

serving suggestion Serve with a bowl of chopped pineapple, apple and orange segments.

cheesy polenta *muffins* with tomato jam

preparation time 25 minutes ■ cooking time 45 minutes

2 bacon rashers, chopped finely
$1\frac{1}{2}$ cups (225g) self-raising flour
1 cup (170g) polenta
$\frac{1}{2}$ teaspoon bicarbonate of soda
$\frac{1}{2}$ teaspoon salt
1 tablespoon caster sugar
3 green onions, chopped coarsely
$\frac{1}{4}$ cup coarsely chopped fresh flat-leaf parsley
1 cup (125g) coarsely grated cheddar cheese
1 egg
1 cup (250ml) buttermilk

TOMATO JAM

5 small tomatoes (650g), chopped coarsely
2 medium brown onions (300g), chopped coarsely
3 red thai chillies, seeded, chopped coarsely
4 cloves garlic, chopped coarsely
$\frac{1}{2}$ cup (125ml) malt vinegar
$\frac{1}{2}$ cup (100g) firmly packed brown sugar
1 tablespoon tomato paste

1. Make tomato jam according to instructions below.
2. Preheat oven to moderate. Grease 12-hole ($\frac{1}{3}$ cup/80ml) muffin pan.
3. Cook bacon, stirring, in heated medium non-stick frying pan until crisp; drain on absorbent paper.
4. Place bacon in large bowl with remaining muffin ingredients; stir until just combined. Spoon mixture evenly into prepared pan; bake, uncovered, in moderate oven about 35 minutes. Serve muffins with tomato jam.

tomato jam Combine ingredients in medium saucepan. Bring to a boil, stirring; simmer, uncovered, about 45 minutes or until mixture thickens, stirring occasionally. Blend or process tomato mixture until pureed.

SERVES 6

per serving 11.7g fat; 1990kJ

tip Muffins can be made a day ahead and refrigerated, covered (you can also freeze them for up to three months). Wrap in foil and reheat briefly in a hot oven before serving. The tomato jam can be made three days ahead and refrigerated, covered.

serving suggestion Serve with creamy scrambled eggs.

chorizo, potato and basil *frittata*

preparation time 10 minutes ■ cooking time 45 minutes (plus cooling time)

2 medium potatoes (400g), halved
250g chorizo sausages, chopped finely
6 eggs, beaten lightly
½ cup (125ml) cream
3 green onions, chopped coarsely
2 teaspoons finely chopped fresh basil leaves

1 Preheat oven to moderate.

2 Grease deep 20cm-round cake pan; line base and side with baking paper.

3 Boil, steam or microwave potato until just tender; drain. Cool; slice thinly.

4 Cook chorizo in heated small non-stick frying pan, stirring, until chorizo is browned all over; drain on absorbent paper.

5 Layer half the potato over base of prepared pan; top with half the chorizo. Repeat with remaining potato and chorizo. Pour in the combined egg, cream, onion and basil; bake, uncovered, in moderate oven about 30 minutes or until frittata sets and is browned lightly.

SERVES 8

per serving 20g fat; 1127kJ

tip You can cook the frittata on top of the stove, in an oiled medium, high-sided frying pan; cook on low heat, uncovered, until almost set, then brown frittata under a preheated grill.

serving suggestion Serve with oven-roasted tomatoes.

eggs benedict

preparation time 20 minutes
cooking time 30 minutes (plus cooling time)

Classic eggs benedict (toasted English muffin halves, poached eggs with runny yolks, crisp Canadian bacon and lemony hollandaise sauce) is thought to have originated during the 1920s when a Wall Street financier by the name of Benedict complained to the chef at Manhattan's famous Delmonico's restaurant that he was bored with the menu. This dish was the chef's attempt to placate his regular (and very rich) customer. Canadian bacon, made from meaty pork loin rather than the usual belly, trimmed of all fat and cured like ham, isn't of Canadian origin – there it is called back bacon – but is eaten throughout all of North America in general. We have substituted finely shaved leg ham, trimmed of all fat, for the Canadian bacon in this version.

8 eggs
8 english muffins
200g shaved ham

HOLLANDAISE SAUCE

1/4 cup (60ml) white wine vinegar
3 black peppercorns
1 bay leaf
2 egg yolks
125g butter, melted
1 teaspoon lemon juice

1. Poach eggs, in batches, in large frying pan of simmering water, uncovered, until cooked as desired; drain on absorbent paper.
2. Meanwhile, split muffins in half; toast until just crisp and browned lightly.
3. Place two muffin halves on each serving plate; layer ham on one muffin half. Top with an egg and hollandaise sauce.

hollandaise sauce Combine vinegar, peppercorns and bay leaf in small saucepan; bring to a boil. Simmer, uncovered, until reduced by half. Strain into small jug; cool. Blend or process egg yolks until smooth. With motor operating, gradually add 1 teaspoon of the melted butter (it must be bubbling hot) to yolks; blend or process until mixture starts to thicken. Then, with motor operating, add 2 teaspoons of the vinegar mixture at a time, alternating with 2 teaspoons of the remaining melted butter, processing until sauce thickens and all butter and vinegar have been incorporated; stir in juice.

SERVES 8

per serving 21.3g fat; 1527kJ

tip If the hollandaise sauce curdles, gradually stir in 2 tablespoons of boiling water.

serving suggestion Substitute the ham with just-wilted fresh spinach to make that other breakfast favourite, eggs florentine; serve either version with browned potatoes and a jug of mimosas (champagne and orange juice) or bloody marys.

bircher *muesli*

preparation time 15 minutes (plus refrigeration time)

During the late 19th century, a Swiss nutritionist, Dr Max Bircher-Benner, developed a breakfast cereal for his patients. A staunch vegetarian, Bircher-Benner believed firmly that people should eat as little processed food as possible. Bircher muesli has become a very popular breakfast food and is now being made commercially by a few yogurt and cereal companies.

3 cups (270g) rolled oats
2 cups (500ml) fresh orange juice
400g yogurt
1 cup (160g) seeded dried dates, chopped coarsely
1/2 cup (85g) raisins
1/2 cup (150g) dried apricots, sliced thinly
1/3 cup (80ml) honey
1 cup (250ml) milk
1 large apple (200g), peeled, grated coarsely
1/3 cup (45g) toasted slivered almonds

1. Combine oats, juice and yogurt in large bowl. Cover tightly; refrigerate overnight.
2. Stir dates, raisins, apricot, honey, milk and apple into oat mixture. Cover; refrigerate 30 minutes.
3. Serve muesli in individual serving bowls; top with almonds.

SERVES 6

per serving 12.6g fat; 2000kJ

tips Try to find plain full-cream yogurt, sometimes called country-style or Greek-style, for this recipe. Other types, especially the low-fat kind, are not suitable.

Additional milk can be added if muesli is too thick.

Use a tart, crisp green apple, such as a granny smith, for this recipe.

serving suggestion Serve muesli topped with a combination of fresh mixed berries.

smoked salmon on buckwheat pancakes with herbed crème fraîche

preparation time 20 minutes (plus refrigeration time) ■ cooking time 15 minutes

You need 12 pancakes for this recipe.

$1/2$ cup (75g) buckwheat flour
$3/4$ cup (110g) self-raising flour
1 tablespoon caster sugar
$1/4$ teaspoon bicarbonate of soda
1 egg, beaten lightly
1 cup (250ml) milk
200g baby spinach leaves
400g smoked salmon, sliced

HERBED CRÈME FRAÎCHE

200g crème fraîche
1 tablespoon finely chopped fresh garlic chives
1 tablespoon finely chopped fresh dill
1 green onion, chopped finely
1 tablespoon drained capers, chopped finely

1 Sift flours, sugar and soda into large bowl; gradually whisk in combined egg and milk until mixture is smooth. Cover; refrigerate 30 minutes.

2 Pour 2 tablespoons of batter for each pancake in heated medium non-stick frying pan; cook, in batches, until browned lightly both sides.

3 Meanwhile, boil, steam or microwave spinach until just wilted. Drain; pat dry with absorbent paper.

4 Top pancakes with salmon, herbed crème fraîche and spinach.

herbed crème fraîche Combine ingredients in small bowl.

SERVES 6

per serving 12.9g fat; 1319kJ

tips You can use sour cream if crème fraîche isn't available. Herbed crème fraîche can be made a day ahead and refrigerated, covered.

Pancake batter can be made a day ahead and refrigerated, covered.

serving suggestion Serve with a jug of freshly squeezed orange juice.

finger food

kumara and pea *samosas* with cucumber yogurt

preparation time 1 hour ■ cooking time 50 minutes

Samosas are Indian savoury deep-fried pastries filled with vegetables or meat, or a combination of both.

1 medium potato (200g), chopped coarsely
1 medium kumara (400g), chopped coarsely
1 cup (125g) frozen peas
20g ghee
1 medium brown onion (150g), chopped finely
1 clove garlic, crushed
2 teaspoons grated fresh ginger
1 teaspoon ground cumin
1/2 teaspoon ground coriander
1/4 teaspoon garam masala
6 sheets ready-rolled puff pastry
vegetable oil, for deep-frying

CUCUMBER YOGURT

1 lebanese cucumber (130g), seeded, chopped coarsely
1 tablespoon coarsely chopped fresh mint leaves
200g yogurt
1 clove garlic, quartered
1 tablespoon lemon juice

1 Boil, steam or microwave potato, kumara and peas, separately, until tender; drain.

2 Meanwhile, heat ghee in medium frying pan; cook onion, garlic and ginger, stirring, until onion is soft. Add spices; cook, stirring, until fragrant.

3 Mash potato and kumara together in large bowl until almost smooth. Add peas and onion mixture; stir to combine.

4 Using a 7.5cm cutter, cut nine rounds from each pastry sheet. Place 1 heaped teaspoon of filling in centre of each round; pinch edges together to seal.

5 Heat oil in wok or large saucepan; deep-fry samosas, in batches, until browned all over. Drain on absorbent paper; serve with cucumber yogurt.

cucumber yogurt Blend or process ingredients until combined.

MAKES 54

per serving 2.6g fat; 173kJ

tips As an alternative to deep-frying, bake samosas, uncovered, in a moderate oven about 30 minutes or until browned.

Prepare the samosas to the end of Step 4 then freeze until needed. There's no need to defrost them before cooking; simply remove from the freezer and deep-fry (or oven-bake) until browned all over and heated through.

prawn *wontons* with sweet chilli sauce

preparation time 45 minutes ■ cooking time 20 minutes

1kg medium uncooked prawns
3 green onions, chopped coarsely
1 tablespoon grated fresh ginger
1 clove garlic, quartered
1 tablespoon lime juice
1 tablespoon finely chopped fresh vietnamese mint leaves
1 tablespoon finely chopped fresh thai basil leaves
40 wonton wrappers
1 egg, beaten lightly
1/2 cup (125ml) sweet chilli sauce

1 Shell and devein prawns.

2 Blend or process prawns, onion, ginger, garlic and juice until mixture forms a paste. Stir in mint and basil.

3 Place 1 heaped teaspoon of prawn filling in centre of each wonton wrapper. Brush edges with egg; pinch edges together to seal.

4 Place wontons, in batches, in single layer in bamboo steamer. Cook, covered, over wok or large saucepan of simmering water about 10 minutes or until wontons are cooked through.

5 Serve wontons with chilli sauce.

MAKES 40

per wonton 0.3g fat; 103kJ

tips You can deep-fry wontons in vegetable oil, in batches, until browned all over.

Uncooked wontons are suitable to freeze up to three months. There's no need to defrost them. Remove from freezer and cook in covered bamboo steamer for about 15 minutes or until cooked through.

serving suggestion Serve steamed wontons either using the bamboo steamer as a tray or sit each wonton on a porcelain Chinese soup spoon, drizzle with sweet chilli sauce then pass around on trays to guests.

beetroot dip

preparation time 10 minutes
cooking time 45 minutes

3 medium trimmed beetroot (500g)
1 clove garlic, crushed
200g yogurt
1 teaspoon ground cumin
2 teaspoons lemon juice

1 Cook beetroot in large saucepan of boiling water, uncovered, about 45 minutes or until tender. Drain; cool 5 minutes. Wearing gloves, peel beetroot while warm; chop coarsely.

2 Blend or process beetroot with garlic, yogurt, cumin and juice until smooth.

MAKES 2 CUPS (585g)

per tablespoon 0.3g fat; 63kJ

serving suggestion Serve with crackers, crudités or toasted shards of pitta.

fetta dip

preparation time 10 minutes

200g fetta cheese
3/4 cup (150g) ricotta cheese
2 tablespoons lemon juice
2 tablespoons olive oil
1 clove garlic, quartered

1 Crumble fetta into large bowl; stir in remaining ingredients. Process mixture, in batches, until smooth.

MAKES 1 3/4 CUPS (385g)

per tablespoon 4.8g fat; 225kJ

tips Stir any leftover dip through mashed potatoes.

Add a tablespoon of either finely chopped fresh oregano or mint to the dip.

This recipe can be made up to two days ahead and refrigerated, covered.

serving suggestion Serve with bruschetta or baby spinach leaves.

chicken wing trio

Perfect finger food, chicken wings are so good we've served them three ways.

teriyaki chicken wings

preparation time 20 minutes
(plus marinating time)
cooking time 40 minutes

- 24 chicken wings (approximately 2kg)
- 3/4 cup (180ml) teriyaki sauce
- 2 tablespoons peanut oil
- 2 teaspoons grated fresh ginger
- 2 cloves garlic, crushed
- 1 red thai chilli, seeded, chopped finely
- 1 tablespoon brown sugar
- 1 teaspoon sesame oil
- 1/2 teaspoon five-spice powder
- 1 tablespoon sesame seeds, toasted

1. Cut chicken wings into three pieces at joints; reserve wing tips for another use.
2. Combine sauce, peanut oil, ginger, garlic, chilli, sugar, sesame oil and five-spice in large bowl with chicken; toss to coat chicken in marinade. Cover; refrigerate 3 hours or overnight.
3. Preheat oven to hot. Drain chicken; discard marinade. Place chicken on oiled oven rack over baking dish; roast, uncovered, in hot oven about 40 minutes or until browned and cooked through, turning once during cooking.
4. Serve chicken wings sprinkled with sesame seeds.

MAKES 48

per piece 4.6g fat; 268kJ

honey-vindaloo glazed chicken wings

preparation time 15 minutes
(plus marinating time)
cooking time 40 minutes

- 24 chicken wings (approximately 2kg)
- 1/3 cup (80ml) honey
- 2 tablespoons vindaloo curry paste
- 1/3 cup (80ml) soy sauce
- 2 tablespoons peanut oil

1. Cut chicken wings into three pieces at joints; reserve wing tips for another use.
2. Combine remaining ingredients in large bowl with chicken; toss to coat chicken in marinade. Cover; refrigerate 3 hours or overnight.
3. Preheat oven to hot. Place undrained chicken on oiled oven rack over baking dish; roast, uncovered, in hot oven about 40 minutes or until browned and cooked through, turning once during cooking.

MAKES 48

per piece 4.5g fat; 285kJ

masala-crusted chicken wings

preparation time 15 minutes
(plus marinating time)
cooking time 45 minutes

- 1 tablespoon ground cumin
- 2 teaspoons ground coriander
- 1 teaspoon ground turmeric
- 1/2 teaspoon chilli powder
- 2 teaspoons garam masala
- 1 teaspoon finely grated lemon rind
- 2 tablespoons lemon juice
- 1/4 cup (60ml) peanut oil
- 24 chicken wings (approximately 2kg)

1. Heat medium dry frying pan; cook spices, stirring, over low heat, until fragrant.
2. Combine spices in large bowl with rind, juice and oil.
3. Cut chicken wings into three pieces at joints; reserve wing tips for another use.
4. Add chicken to spice mixture; toss to coat chicken in marinade. Cover; refrigerate 3 hours or overnight.
5. Preheat oven to hot. Place undrained chicken on oiled oven rack over baking dish; roast, uncovered, in hot oven about 40 minutes or until browned and cooked through, turning once during cooking.

MAKES 48

per piece 4.8g fat; 273kJ

tips Wing tips can be used to make stock.

You can freeze the marinated chicken and cook at a later date, if you prefer. Place marinated chicken in a storage container or freezer bag; seal and freeze up to six months.

opposite: masala-crusted chicken wings (left); teriyaki chicken wings (centre); honey-vindaloo glazed chicken wings (right)

peking duck *crepes*

preparation time 1 hour (plus refrigeration time) ■ cooking time 30 minutes

Peking-style barbecued ducks are available ready-to-eat from specialist Asian food outlets.

1 cup (150g) plain flour
1/2 teaspoon salt
1 egg, beaten lightly
2 cups (500ml) milk
200g garlic chives
1 chinese barbecued duck
2 tablespoons hoisin sauce
2 tablespoons plum sauce
2 lebanese cucumbers (260g), seeded, sliced thinly into 4cm lengths

1 Combine flour and salt in medium bowl; gradually whisk in combined egg and milk until mixture is smooth. Strain mixture into large jug.

2 Finely chop enough chives to make 1/4 cup chopped chives; reserve remaining chives. Stir chopped chives into batter. Cover; refrigerate 1 hour.

3 Meanwhile, remove skin and meat from duck; discard bones. Remove and discard excess fat from under meat and skin, then slice both as thinly as possible.

4 Pour 1/4 cup batter into heated oiled 20cm non-stick frying pan; cook crepe until browned lightly both sides. Repeat with remaining batter; you should have 11 crepes when finished.

5 Using an 8cm cutter, cut three rounds from each crepe. Spread each small crepe with an equal amount of combined sauces; top with duck and cucumber.

6 Place reserved chives in small heatproof bowl; cover with boiling water. Stand until chives are wilted; drain. Fold in edges of crepes; roll to enclose filling. Tie a chive around each crepe to secure; trim ends.

Each large crepe will give you three smaller ones

Fill crepes with equal amounts of the filling ingredients

Tuck in the sides of the rolls after the first complete turn

MAKES 33

per crepe 4.4g fat; 310kJ

tip Crepes, without filling, are suitable to freeze. Place pieces of plastic wrap or baking paper between each crepe before freezing, so they don't stick together.

sushi selection

Here are four easy varieties of sushi you can make in no time. First, make the sushi rice, then, when it is cooling, prepare the various filling ingredients so that you can assemble each part of the quartet at the same time. This amount of sushi rice is enough for the four recipes that follow. Serve sushi accompanied by separate small bowls of Japanese soy sauce, thinly sliced pickled ginger and wasabi.

sushi *rice*

preparation time 5 minutes ■ cooking time 15 minutes (plus standing time)

1½ cups (300g) koshihikari rice
¼ cup (60ml) rice wine vinegar
1 teaspoon salt
1½ tablespoons sugar
1½ tablespoons mirin

Add rice to large saucepan of boiling water; boil, uncovered, until just tender. Drain; stand rice 5 minutes. Stir in combined vinegar, salt, sugar and mirin; cool.

tip If you can't find koshihikari rice, you can use calrose or arborio rice.

Each of the four sushi rolls following requires a quarter of the given amount of cooled sushi rice. You will also need some of the following for use among each of the four kinds of sushi rolls:

1 lebanese cucumber (130g), halved lengthways, seeded, then cut into 1cm long strips
1 small carrot (70g), cut into 1cm long strips
1 small avocado (200g), cut into 1cm slices

smoked *salmon* roll

preparation time 10 minutes

Wasabi is a green Asian horseradish used to make a fiery sauce traditionally served with Japanese raw fish dishes.

1 sheet toasted nori
¼ portion sushi rice (above)
¼ teaspoon wasabi
1 slice smoked salmon (15g), halved
2 slices avocado
1 teaspoon coarsely chopped fresh dill

1. Place nori sheet, rough-side up, on dampened bamboo sushi mat. Wet fingers; spread rice over nori, leaving 4cm-gap on short side furthest from you. Press rice firmly in place; use finger to make long indentation across rice edge closest to you.
2. Place wasabi, salmon, avocado and dill in indentation. Use empty edge of mat to help start rolling sushi; press mat firmly as you roll. Carefully remove roll from mat; using sharp wet knife, cut roll into eight pieces.

SERVES 8

per serving 0.8g fat; 117kJ

easy steps to sensational sushi

Spreading cooled rice on nori

Marking indentation on the rice with finger

Placing filling components in hollow of rice

Rolling mat firmly around filled nori

vegetarian roll

preparation time 10 minutes (plus soaking time) ■ cooking time 5 minutes

Daikon radishes are an everyday fixture at the Japanese table. This long, white horseradish has a wonderful, sweet flavour and is used in stir-fries and raw in salads; it is also sliced and pickled in soy sauce and sugar and often eaten with fish. You can purchase whole pickled daikon at Asian food outlets.

2 teaspoons peanut oil
1 egg, beaten lightly
1 large dried shiitake mushroom
1 sheet toasted nori
1/4 portion sushi rice (page 20)
1/4 teaspoon wasabi
2 strips lebanese cucumber
2 teaspoons finely sliced pickled ginger
40g finely sliced pickled daikon

1. Heat oil in wok or large frying pan. Cook egg; swirl wok so egg forms a thin omelette over base. Cook omelette until set; remove from wok. Cool; roll omelette firmly. Cut into thin slices.
2. Place mushroom in small heatproof bowl; cover with boiling water. Stand until tender; drain. Discard stem; slice cap as thinly as possible.
3. Place nori sheet, rough-side up, on dampened bamboo sushi mat. Wet fingers; spread rice over nori, leaving 4cm-gap on short side furthest from you. Press rice firmly in place; use finger to make long indentation across rice edge closest to you.
4. Place wasabi, omelette, mushroom, cucumber, ginger and daikon in indentation. Use empty edge of mat to help start rolling sushi; press mat firmly as you roll. Carefully remove roll from mat; using sharp wet knife, cut roll into eight pieces.

SERVES 8

per serving 2g fat; 172kJ

teriyaki *chicken* roll

preparation time 10 minutes (plus soaking time)

You can either poach a small chicken thigh fillet or use some of the meat from a purchased barbecued chicken for this recipe.

- 1/4 cup (40g) shredded cooked chicken
- 1 teaspoon teriyaki sauce
- 1 dried shiitake mushroom
- 1 sheet toasted nori
- 1/4 portion sushi rice (page 20)
- 1/4 teaspoon wasabi
- 2 strips lebanese cucumber
- 2 strips carrot

1. Combine chicken and sauce in small bowl.
2. Place mushroom in small heatproof bowl; cover with boiling water. Stand until tender; drain. Discard stem; slice mushroom cap as thinly as possible.
3. Place nori sheet, rough-side up, on dampened bamboo sushi mat. Wet fingers; spread rice over nori, leaving 4cm-gap on short side furthest from you. Press rice firmly in place; use finger to make long indentation across rice edge closest to you.
4. Place wasabi, chicken mixture, mushroom, cucumber and carrot in indentation. Use empty edge of mat to help start rolling sushi; press mat firmly as you roll. Carefully remove roll from mat; using sharp wet knife, cut roll into eight pieces.

SERVES 8

per serving 0.3g fat; 120kJ

california roll

preparation time 10 minutes

- 1 teaspoon mayonnaise
- 1/4 teaspoon wasabi
- 1 sheet toasted nori
- 1/4 portion sushi rice (page 20)
- 1 crab stick, cut in half lengthways
- 2 slices avocado
- 1 strip carrot
- 2 strips lebanese cucumber

1. Combine mayonnaise and wasabi in small bowl.
2. Place nori sheet, rough-side up, on dampened bamboo sushi mat. Wet fingers; spread rice over nori, leaving 4cm-gap on short side furthest from you. Press rice firmly in place; use finger to make long indentation across rice edge closest to you.
3. Place mayonnaise mixture, crab, avocado, carrot and cucumber in indentation. Use empty edge of mat to help start rolling sushi; press mat firmly as you roll. Carefully remove roll from mat; using sharp wet knife, cut roll into eight pieces.

SERVES 8

per serving 0.9g fat; 129kJ

starters

mediterranean grilled vegetables with tomato vinaigrette

preparation time 20 minutes (plus standing time)
cooking time 1 hour

You need approximately 1.5kg of untrimmed fresh beetroot for this recipe.

5 medium trimmed beetroot (825g)
4 large egg tomatoes (360g), halved
cooking-oil spray
2 medium eggplants (600g)
1 tablespoon salt
6 medium flat mushrooms (600g)
1/4 cup (60ml) olive oil
2 tablespoons white wine vinegar
1 teaspoon salt, extra
300g fetta cheese, crumbled
1/2 cup loosely packed fresh basil leaves

1. Preheat oven to hot.
2. Wrap beetroot individually in foil; place in baking dish. Bake in hot oven about 50 minutes or until tender; cool 5 minutes. Wearing gloves, peel while still warm; cut beetroot into 1cm slices.
3. Meanwhile, place tomato halves on oiled oven tray; coat with cooking-oil spray. Bake in hot oven about 40 minutes or until browned lightly.
4. Cut eggplant into 1cm slices; place in colander. Sprinkle with salt; stand 30 minutes. Rinse eggplant under cold water; drain on absorbent paper.
5. Cook eggplant and mushrooms, in batches, on heated oiled grill plate (or grill or barbecue) until browned both sides.
6. Blend or process tomato with oil, vinegar and extra salt until pureed. Push tomato vinaigrette through food mill or fine sieve into large bowl; discard pulp.
7. Divide tomato vinaigrette among serving plates; top with mushroom, eggplant, beetroot, cheese and basil.

SERVES 6

per serving 22.5g fat; 1549kJ

tip Tomato vinaigrette mixture can be made a day ahead and refrigerated, covered.

serving suggestion Serve as a starter to a main meal of grilled lamb chops or any meat skewers, and a green salad.

roasted kumara and *rocket salad*

preparation time 15 minutes ■ cooking time 35 minutes

2 medium kumara (800g)
cooking-oil spray
2 tablespoons macadamia nut oil
1 teaspoon sesame oil
2 tablespoons white wine vinegar
2 teaspoons sugar
2 teaspoons dijon mustard
1 tablespoon white sesame seeds, toasted
150g rocket leaves

1. Preheat oven to moderately hot. Chop kumara coarsely.
2. Place kumara on oven tray; coat with cooking-oil spray. Bake in moderately hot oven, uncovered, about 35 minutes or until tender and browned lightly.
3. Combine oils, vinegar, sugar and mustard in screw-top jar; shake well.
4. Gently toss roasted kumara in large bowl with sesame seeds, rocket and macadamia-oil dressing.

SERVES 6

per serving 8.5g fat; 720kJ

tips Mesclun or baby spinach leaves can be used instead of rocket. The dressing can be made a day ahead and refrigerated, covered.

serving suggestion Serve, with toasted pide, as the starter for a roast chicken main course.

oysters with smoked salmon

preparation time 15 minutes

1 lime
80g ricotta cheese
1/4 cup (60g) mayonnaise
(preferably homemade)
2 teaspoons drained capers
36 medium oysters on the half
shell (approximately 2.25kg)
60g smoked salmon, sliced thinly

1. Carefully peel rind from lime; cut rind as thinly as possible (you need 1 tablespoon of thinly sliced rind). Squeeze lime into small bowl (you need 1 tablespoon of lime juice).
2. Blend or process cheese, mayonnaise, juice and capers until mixture is pureed.
3. Top oysters with cheese mixture, then sprinkle with salmon and rind; serve oysters immediately.

SERVES 6

per serving 6.9g fat; 494kJ

tip When peeling the rind from lime, take care not to include any of the pith, the bitter white part of the peel. Keep the slices of rind wrapped in plastic so as not to lose any of the zesty citrus oil.

serving suggestion Serve on a bed of rock salt, also sprinkled with lime rind, before a classic standing rib roast and browned vegetables main course.

vegetable *tempura* with wasabi aioli

preparation time 20 minutes ■ cooking time 10 minutes

Broccolini has a delicate flavour with a subtle, peppery edge, and is milder and sweeter than traditional broccoli. It is completely edible from flower to stem. This strikingly versatile vegetable is a cross between broccoli and chinese kale, and is sometimes known as baby broccoli.

2 medium carrots (240g)
1 medium red capsicum (200g)
1 medium green capsicum (200g)
1 large brown onion (200g)
2 egg whites
1 cup (150g) plain flour
½ cup (75g) cornflour
1¼ cups (310ml) iced water
vegetable oil, for deep-frying
800g butternut pumpkin, sliced thinly
400g broccolini
½ cup (125ml) soy sauce

WASABI AIOLI

2 egg yolks
1 tablespoon lemon juice
1 tablespoon wasabi
1 clove garlic, quartered
½ cup (125ml) vegetable oil
1 tablespoon hot water

1. Using a vegetable peeler, cut carrots into long thin ribbons. Halve capsicums; discard seeds and membranes. Cut capsicum into 2cm-thick slices. Cut onion into thin wedges.
2. Just before serving, whisk egg whites in small bowl until soft peaks form. Sift flours into large bowl. Stir in the water; fold in egg white.
3. Heat oil in wok or large frying pan. Dip vegetables, one piece at a time, in batter; deep-fry until browned lightly and crisp. Drain on absorbent paper; keep each batch warm as you deep-fry remainder. Serve tempura with separate bowls of the soy sauce and wasabi aioli.

wasabi aioli Blend or process egg yolks, juice, wasabi and garlic until smooth. With motor operating, add oil gradually in thin stream; process until mixture thickens. Thin aioli with the hot water, if desired.

SERVES 6

per serving 40g fat; 2407kJ

tips Tempura batter must be made just before required. Do not overmix the batter – it should be lumpy.

Wasabi aioli is also delicious when served as a dip for raw vegetables or stirred into a fish soup.

serving suggestion Serve as a first course to a Japanese main meal such as assorted sushi or homemade udon soup.

tuna and avocado

rice paper rolls

preparation time 30 minutes ■ cooking time 50 minutes

Use any raw tuna that's sold as "sashimi" tuna, but bear in mind that you are eating this fish uncooked; smoked salmon or smoked trout can be substituted if you do not want to use raw tuna.

3 medium trimmed beetroot (500g)
12 x 22cm rice paper sheets
12 slices sashimi tuna (200g)
200g snow pea sprouts
4 green onions, sliced thinly
1 large avocado (320g), sliced thinly
70g drained pickled ginger
½ cup (125ml) soy sauce

1 Preheat oven to hot.

2 Wrap trimmed beetroot individually in foil; place in baking dish. Bake in hot oven about 50 minutes or until tender; cool 5 minutes. Wearing gloves, peel while warm; slice thinly.

3 Carefully dip one sheet of the rice paper in medium bowl of warm water until just softened; lift from water carefully, place on board. Place one piece of the tuna in centre of rice paper; top with some of the beetroot, sprouts, onion, avocado and ginger. Roll to enclose filling, folding in ends after first complete turn of the roll. Repeat with remaining rice paper sheets, tuna, beetroot, sprouts, onion, avocado and ginger.

4 Serve rolls accompanied by soy sauce for dipping.

MAKES 12

per serving 4.9g fat; 384kJ

tips Substitute fresh raw salmon or ocean trout fillet for the tuna.

Daikon sprouts, the young shoots of the daikon radish, could be substituted for the snow pea sprouts.

steamed garlic and herb *mussels*

preparation time 30 minutes ■ cooking time 25 minutes

80 medium black mussels (approximately 2kg)
2 tablespoons olive oil
8 cloves garlic, crushed
4 red thai chillies, seeded, chopped finely
1 tablespoon finely grated lemon rind
1 cup (250ml) lemon juice
1 cup (250ml) dry white wine
1/2 cup finely chopped fresh flat-leaf parsley
1/3 cup finely chopped fresh basil leaves

1 Scrub mussels; remove beards.

2 Heat oil in large saucepan; cook garlic, chilli and rind, stirring, about 2 minutes or until fragrant. Add mussels, juice and wine; bring to a boil. Cook, covered, about 5 minutes or until mussels open (discard any that do not). Remove mussels from pan.

3 Bring pan liquid to a boil; cook, uncovered, about 10 minutes or until mixture thickens slightly. Stir in parsley and basil.

4 Return mussels to pan; simmer, stirring, until heated through.

SERVES 8

per serving 5.9g fat; 514kJ
serving suggestion Serve with steamed jasmine or basmati rice.

stir-fried
garlic prawns

preparation time 15 minutes ■ cooking time 5 minutes

24 large uncooked king prawns (approximately 1.25kg)
1/3 cup (80ml) olive oil
6 cloves garlic, crushed
2 red thai chillies, seeded, chopped finely
2 tablespoons finely chopped fresh flat-leaf parsley

1. Shell and devein prawns, leaving tails intact.
2. Heat oil in wok or large frying pan; stir-fry garlic and chilli until fragrant.
3. Add prawns; stir-fry until just changed in colour. Serve sprinkled with parsley.

SERVES 4

per serving 19.9 fat; 1186kJ

tip If you're planning a barbecue, you can marinate the prawns in the remaining ingredients overnight, then thread onto skewers and barbecue.

serving suggestion Serve with lemon wedges, crusty bread, and perhaps steamed rice and a tomato and avocado salad.

light lunches

tandoori *lamb* cutlets with cucumber salad

preparation time 25 minutes (plus marinating time) ■ cooking time 20 minutes

200g yogurt
2 cloves garlic, quartered
1 large brown onion (200g), chopped coarsely
2 tablespoons grated fresh ginger
1/4 cup (60ml) lemon juice
1 teaspoon chilli powder
2 teaspoons garam masala
1 tablespoon sweet paprika
2 teaspoons ground cumin
12 french-trimmed lamb cutlets (approximately 1kg)

CUCUMBER SALAD

2 small green cucumbers (260g)
2 red thai chillies, seeded, chopped finely
1/4 cup (60ml) peanut oil
1 1/2 tablespoons lemon juice
1 clove garlic, crushed
2 teaspoons cumin seeds, toasted
1 tablespoon finely shredded mint leaves

CORIANDER YOGURT

1/2 cup loosely packed coriander leaves
200g yogurt

1. Blend or process yogurt, garlic, onion, ginger, juice and spices until pureed.
2. Pour tandoori marinade over lamb in large bowl; stir to coat well. Cover; refrigerate overnight.
3. Cook undrained lamb, in batches, on heated oiled grill plate (or grill or barbecue) until browned both sides and cooked as desired.
4. Serve lamb with cucumber salad and coriander yogurt.

cucumber salad Using a vegetable peeler, peel cucumber into long thin ribbons. Just before serving, gently toss cucumber with remaining ingredients in medium bowl.

coriander yogurt Blend or process coriander and yogurt until combined.

SERVES 6

per serving 18.1g fat; 1200kJ

tip The tandoori marinade can also be used with poultry and seafood. It can be made up to two days ahead and refrigerated, covered.

serving suggestion Drizzle with lemon juice just before serving and accompany with fresh naan.

fettuccine in creamy mushroom sauce

preparation time 15 minutes ■ cooking time 30 minutes

500g fettuccine
1 tablespoon olive oil
1 large brown onion (200g), chopped finely
2 cloves garlic, crushed
400g button mushrooms, halved
400g swiss brown mushrooms, quartered
1 cup (250ml) chicken stock
1 cup (250ml) dry white wine
300ml cream
2 tablespoons seeded mustard
2 tablespoons coarsely chopped fresh oregano

1 Cook pasta in large saucepan of boiling water, uncovered, until just tender; drain.

2 Meanwhile, heat oil in large saucepan; cook onion and garlic, stirring, until onion is soft. Add mushrooms; cook, stirring, about 10 minutes or until mushrooms are browned and tender.

3 Stir in stock and wine; simmer, uncovered, about 5 minutes or until reduced by half. Stir in cream, mustard and half of the oregano; bring to a boil. Simmer, uncovered, 2 minutes.

4 Add pasta; toss to reheat. Sprinkle with remaining oregano.

SERVES 6

per serving 13.3g fat; 1753kJ

tip Swiss brown mushrooms are sometimes sold as roman, portobello or cremini mushrooms; you can substitute them with flat, oyster or enoki mushrooms, if you prefer.

serving suggestion Serve with a mixed green salad.

carrot and roasted red capsicum *soup*

preparation time 25 minutes ■ cooking time 1 hour 30 minutes

4 large red capsicums (1.4kg)
1 tablespoon olive oil
2 medium brown onions (300g), chopped coarsely
2 cloves garlic, crushed
2 tablespoons grated fresh ginger
1 teaspoon ground coriander
1 teaspoon cumin seeds
3 large carrots (540g), chopped coarsely
2 large potatoes (600g), chopped coarsely
2 x 400g cans tomatoes
1.5 litres (6 cups) water
200g yogurt

1 Quarter capsicums; remove and discard seeds and membrane. Roast under grill or in very hot oven, skin-side up, until skin blisters and blackens. Cover capsicum quarters in plastic or paper for 5 minutes; peel away and discard skin, then chop coarsely.

2 Heat oil in large saucepan; cook onion and garlic, stirring, until onion softens. Add ginger, coriander and seeds; cook, stirring, until fragrant.

3 Add capsicum, carrot and potato; cook, stirring, 5 minutes. Stir in undrained crushed tomatoes and the water. Bring to a boil; simmer, covered, about 1 hour or until carrot and potato are soft.

4 Blend or process soup, in batches, until pureed. Push through food mill or strainer into same cleaned pan. Reheat until soup is hot; spoon yogurt on top and serve. Sprinkle with additional cumin seeds, if desired.

SERVES 8

per serving 4.1g fat; 706kJ

tips Instead of covering roasted capsicum in plastic or paper, you can place an inverted bowl over the roasted capsicum to create a steamy environment before peeling.

Having a big batch of soup in the freezer is always a great stand-by when friends drop in unexpectedly. You can freeze this soup (without yogurt) for up to three months. Make this recipe and then cool soup for 10 minutes; place in storage container and refrigerate, covered, until cold; place in freezer.

serving suggestion Serve with cornmeal muffins and olive tapenade.

prawns with curly endive

preparation time 40 minutes (plus marinating time)
cooking time 10 minutes

Daikon radishes are an everyday fixture at the Japanese table. This long, white horseradish has a wonderful, sweet flavour and is used in stir-fries and raw in salads; it is also pickled in soy sauce and sugar and often eaten with fish. You can purchase daikon at Asian food outlets.

48 medium uncooked prawns (1.2kg)
4 cloves garlic, crushed
1 teaspoon wasabi
2 tablespoons water
2 tablespoons mirin
2 tablespoons dark soy sauce
1 tablespoon seasoned rice vinegar
2 teaspoons sugar
1 small daikon (400g)
200g snow peas, sliced thinly
4 green onions, chopped coarsely
100g tat soi leaves, torn
1 baby cos lettuce, torn
100g curly endive
1 large cucumber (400g), seeded, sliced thinly
2 tablespoons finely sliced pickled ginger
2 tablespoons white sesame seeds, toasted

1 Shell and devein prawns, leaving tails intact. Place prawns in large bowl.

2 Combine garlic and wasabi with the water, mirin, sauce, vinegar and sugar in small bowl. Pour half of the garlic marinade over prawns, cover; refrigerate 3 hours or overnight. Cover and refrigerate remaining garlic marinade.

3 Cut daikon into matchstick-size pieces.

4 Drain prawns; discard marinade. Cook prawns, in batches, in large oiled frying pan until just changed in colour.

5 Combine prawns, daikon, snow peas, onion, tat soi, lettuce, endive, cucumber and ginger in large bowl. Drizzle with reserved garlic marinade; sprinkle with sesame seeds.

SERVES 8

per serving 2.7g fat; 514kJ

tip Tails are left on prawns merely for decorative purposes: remove them when you shell the prawns, if desired.

serving suggestion Serve with fresh french bread.

pizza
with prosciutto and ricotta

preparation time 15 minutes ■ cooking time 15 minutes

3 medium egg tomatoes (225g)
3 x 335g pizza bases
1/2 cup (135g) tomato paste
300g baby spinach leaves
1 large red onion (300g), sliced thinly
9 slices prosciutto (135g), halved
1/4 cup loosely packed, coarsely chopped fresh basil leaves
1 1/2 cups (300g) ricotta cheese
1/4 cup (40g) pine nuts
1/4 cup (60ml) olive oil
2 cloves garlic, crushed

1. Preheat oven to very hot. Cut each tomato into eight wedges.
2. Place pizza bases on oven trays. Spread each base with a third of the tomato paste; top with equal amounts of the tomato, spinach, onion, prosciutto, basil, cheese and nuts. Drizzle each pizza with equal amounts of combined oil and garlic.
3. Bake, uncovered, in very hot oven about 15 minutes or until pizza top is browned lightly and base crisp.

SERVES 6

per serving 27.6g fat; 2934kJ

tip You can buy ready-made packaged pizza bases in two sizes: the large ones we've used here measure 25cm across; smaller ones measure 15cm across and come packaged in pairs with a total weight of 225g. Use six of the small ones to make individual pizzettes.

serving suggestion Serve with a rocket and parmesan salad.

chicken thyme curry

preparation time 15 minutes ■ cooking time 45 minutes

2 tablespoons peanut oil
4 large brown onions (800g), sliced thinly
2 teaspoons finely chopped fresh thyme
1/4 cup (60g) mild curry powder
6 cloves garlic, crushed
1 tablespoon grated fresh ginger
4 medium tomatoes (760g), chopped coarsely
1/4 cup loosely packed, finely chopped fresh coriander leaves
1.5kg chicken thigh fillets
2 cups (500ml) chicken stock

1 Heat oil in large saucepan; cook onion, thyme, curry powder, garlic and ginger, stirring, until onion is soft.

2 Add tomato and coriander; cook, stirring about 5 minutes or until tomato is soft.

3 Cut each thigh fillet into quarters; add to pan. Cook, stirring, about 10 minutes or until chicken is browned lightly. Stir in stock; simmer, uncovered, stirring occasionally, about 15 minutes or until chicken is cooked through and sauce thickens.

SERVES 6

per serving 18.7g fat; 1919kJ

tip This curry is best made a day ahead, so the flavours develop, and refrigerated, covered. It's also suitable to freeze, which means you can defrost and reheat it on the day friends are coming to dinner.

serving suggestion Serve with steamed basmati rice.

marinated octopus *salad*

preparation time 25 minutes (plus marinating time) ■ cooking time 20 minutes

- 2kg cleaned baby octopus
- 3 cups (750ml) water
- 3 cups (750ml) dry white wine
- 4 sprigs fresh flat-leaf parsley
- 3 sprigs fresh oregano
- 2 bay leaves
- 100g snow pea sprouts
- 150g baby spinach leaves
- 4 medium egg tomatoes (300g), seeded, sliced thinly
- 1 medium red onion (170g), sliced thinly

HERB DRESSING

- 1 cup (250ml) olive oil
- 2/3 cup (160ml) lemon juice
- 2 cloves garlic, crushed
- 2/3 cup loosely packed, coarsely chopped fresh flat-leaf parsley
- 2 tablespoons coarsely chopped fresh oregano
- 1/4 cup (60ml) balsamic vinegar

1 Cut octopus in half; combine with the water, wine, parsley, oregano and bay leaves in large saucepan. Bring to a boil; simmer, covered, about 15 minutes or until octopus is tender. Drain; discard herbs, cool octopus.

2 Combine octopus and herb dressing in large bowl. Cover tightly; refrigerate overnight.

3 Just before serving, add sprouts, spinach, tomato and onion to octopus mixture; toss to combine.

herb dressing Combine ingredients in screw-top jar; shake well.

SERVES 6

per serving 43.1g fat; 2999kJ

tip Octopus must be marinated overnight in the herb dressing to tenderise it.

serving suggestion Serve with lots of warm crusty bread to mop up this delicious dressing.

mediterranean *vegetable loaf*

preparation time 20 minutes (plus standing time)
cooking time 45 minutes

1 large eggplant (500g)
1 tablespoon sea salt
2 medium red capsicums (400g)
400g flat mushrooms
2 small carrots (140g), chopped coarsely
1 teaspoon ground cumin
65g packaged light cream cheese
500g vienna loaf
50g thinly sliced peperoni
1/3 cup firmly packed basil leaves

1. Cut eggplant into 1cm slices; place in colander. Sprinkle with salt; stand 30 minutes. Rinse under cold water; drain on absorbent paper.
2. Meanwhile, quarter capsicums; remove and discard seeds and membrane. Roast, under grill or in very hot oven, skin-side up, until skin blisters and blackens. Cover capsicum pieces in plastic or paper for 5 minutes; peel away and discard skin.
3. Cook eggplant and mushrooms, in batches, on heated oiled grill plate (or grill or barbecue) until browned both sides and tender.
4. Boil, steam or microwave carrot until tender; cool.
5. Cook cumin, stirring, in small heated dry frying pan until fragrant. Blend or process carrot, cumin and cheese until pureed.
6. Preheat oven to moderate.
7. Cut bread in half lengthways; remove and discard soft inside of loaf, leaving a 2cm shell.
8. Spread bread base with carrot mixture; top with half of each of the eggplant, peperoni, basil, capsicum and mushrooms. Repeat with remaining eggplant, peperoni, basil, capsicum and mushrooms. Top with remaining bread; using hands, press loaf firmly together. Tie loaf together at 2cm intervals using kitchen string; wrap in foil.
9. Place loaf on ungreased oven tray; bake in moderate oven about 25 minutes or until loaf is heated through and crisp. Cut into six slices and serve.

SERVES 6

per serving 7.6g fat; 1157kJ

tips Recipe can be made a day ahead and refrigerated, covered.
You can also use a cob loaf, or any type of crusty bread for this recipe.
This dish is great for picnics or while on the road.

serving suggestion Serve with a green salad.

vegetables and udon in

chicken-miso broth

preparation time 20 minutes (plus standing time) ■ cooking time 2 hours 10 minutes

Udon is available fresh and dried, and these Japanese broad white wheat noodles are similar to the ones in homemade chicken noodle soup. Nori are sheets of paper-thin dried black seaweed used in Japanese cooking as a flavouring, garnish or for sushi, while miso, a paste made from cooked, mashed, salted and fermented soy beans, is a common ingredient in soups, sauces and dressings. You can buy these ingredients at Asian food stores and selected supermarkets.

1.5kg chicken bones
5 litres (20 cups) water
2 medium carrots (240g), chopped coarsely
2 trimmed sticks celery (150g), chopped coarsely
4 black peppercorns
2 bay leaves
2 medium brown onions (300g), chopped coarsely
10 dried shiitake mushrooms
1/4 cup (65g) white miso paste
50g piece ginger, sliced thinly
1/4 cup (60ml) soy sauce
600g fresh udon noodles
1 large carrot (180g), sliced finely, extra
4 green onions, sliced finely
2 sheets toasted nori, sliced finely

1. Combine bones, the water, carrot, celery, peppercorns, bay leaves and brown onion in large saucepan; bring to a boil. Simmer, uncovered, 2 hours; strain through muslin-lined strainer into large bowl. Reserve stock; discard bones and vegetables.
2. Meanwhile, place mushrooms in medium heatproof bowl; cover with boiling water. Stand about 20 minutes or until just tender; drain. Discard stems; slice caps thinly.
3. Bring stock to a boil. Add miso, ginger and sauce; simmer, uncovered, 5 minutes.
4. Just before serving, stir in noodles and mushroom; simmer, uncovered, until noodles are just tender. Stir in extra carrot and green onion; sprinkle with nori.

SERVES 6

per serving 2.3g fat; 1228kJ

tips Chicken stock can be made a day ahead and refrigerated, covered. You can also freeze chicken stock for up to six months; store in 1- or 2-cup portions, then thaw only the amount you need for other soups and casseroles.

Dried udon, boiled until tender, can be used, but the cooking time will be longer.

serving suggestion Serve with vegetable and prawn tempura.

pappardelle with chilli and semi-dried tomato sauce

preparation time 15 minutes ■ cooking time 25 minutes

2 medium brown onions (300g), chopped coarsely
2 cloves garlic, quartered
1 cup (150g) semi-dried tomatoes in oil, drained
1/4 cup (70g) tomato paste
2 red thai chillies, seeded, chopped finely
2 cups (500ml) beef stock
375g pappardelle
1/4 cup coarsely chopped fresh flat-leaf parsley

1 Blend or process onion, garlic, tomatoes, paste and chilli until mixture forms a paste.

2 Heat large non-stick frying pan; cook tomato mixture, stirring, 10 minutes. Stir in stock, bring to a boil. Reduce heat; simmer sauce, uncovered, about 10 minutes or until thickened slightly.

3 Cook pasta in large saucepan of boiling water, uncovered, until just tender; drain.

4 Just before serving, gently toss pasta through sauce; sprinkle with parsley. Serve with shaved parmesan, if desired.

SERVES 6

per serving 2.9g fat; 1147kJ

tips Pappardelle is the widest ribbon pasta available but you can use any long pasta such as fettuccine or tagliatelle.

This rich sauce gets even better if made the day before required and refrigerated, covered.

serving suggestion Serve with ciabatta and a simple green salad.

chicken parmesan with basil sauce

preparation time 25 minutes ■ cooking time 20 minutes

2 cups (140g) stale breadcrumbs
1/3 cup (25g) finely grated parmesan cheese
2 tablespoons finely chopped fresh flat-leaf parsley
12 chicken tenderloins (750g)
3/4 cup (110g) plain flour
2 eggs, beaten lightly
250g curly endive
150g rocket leaves

BASIL DRESSING

1 cup firmly packed basil leaves
1/2 cup (125ml) olive oil
1/4 cup (60ml) lemon juice
1 clove garlic, crushed

1. Preheat oven to moderately hot.
2. Combine breadcrumbs, cheese and parsley in medium bowl.
3. Toss chicken, one piece at a time, in flour; shake away excess flour. Dip in egg, then in crumb mixture to coat. Place on oiled oven trays; bake in moderately hot oven, uncovered, about 20 minutes or until browned lightly and cooked through.
4. Serve chicken with endive and rocket; drizzle with basil dressing.

basil dressing Blend or process ingredients until combined.

SERVES 4

per serving 43.8g fat; 3162kJ

tips Make the breadcrumbs out of any stale bread (sourdough or ciabatta are both good) and, when you blend or process the bread to make the crumbs, add the parmesan and parsley at the very end of processing time, pulsing just a few times to combine the three ingredients thoroughly.

Once coated in the crumb mixture, the chicken can be frozen for up to two months. Defrost in microwave then bake following instructions in step 3.

zucchini *potato cake*

with oven-baked ratatouille

preparation time 30 minutes (plus standing time)
cooking time 1 hour 15 minutes

1 large eggplant (500g), chopped coarsely
1 tablespoon salt
1 large red capsicum (350g), chopped coarsely
1 large yellow capsicum (350g), chopped coarsely
1 small yellow zucchini (90g), chopped coarsely
1 small green zucchini (90g), chopped coarsely
6 large egg tomatoes (540g), chopped coarsely
1/4 cup (60ml) olive oil
1/4 cup (60ml) balsamic vinegar
1 clove garlic, crushed
1 tablespoon brown sugar
2 tablespoons finely shredded fresh basil leaves
2 large potatoes (600g), sliced thinly
4 medium green zucchini (480g), grated coarsely, extra
2 eggs, beaten lightly
2 egg whites, beaten lightly
1/2 cup (125ml) cream
1 clove garlic, crushed, extra
4 green onions, chopped finely
1 tablespoon finely chopped fresh dill

1. Preheat oven to hot.
2. Place eggplant in colander; sprinkle with salt. Stand 30 minutes; rinse under cold water. Drain on absorbent paper.
3. Combine eggplant, capsicums, zucchini and tomato in large baking dish; drizzle with combined oil, vinegar, garlic and sugar. Bake in hot oven, uncovered, about 50 minutes or until vegetables are tender. Stir basil into ratatouille.
4. Meanwhile, layer potato and extra zucchini in oiled 20cm x 30cm lamington pan. Pour combined egg, egg white, cream, extra garlic, onion and dill over vegetables; bake, uncovered, in hot oven 25 minutes. Cover; bake about 15 minutes or until potato is tender. Cut potato cake into quarters, then into triangles. Serve with ratatouille.

SERVES 6

per serving 21.1g fat; 1414kJ

tip This dish can be eaten hot or cold.

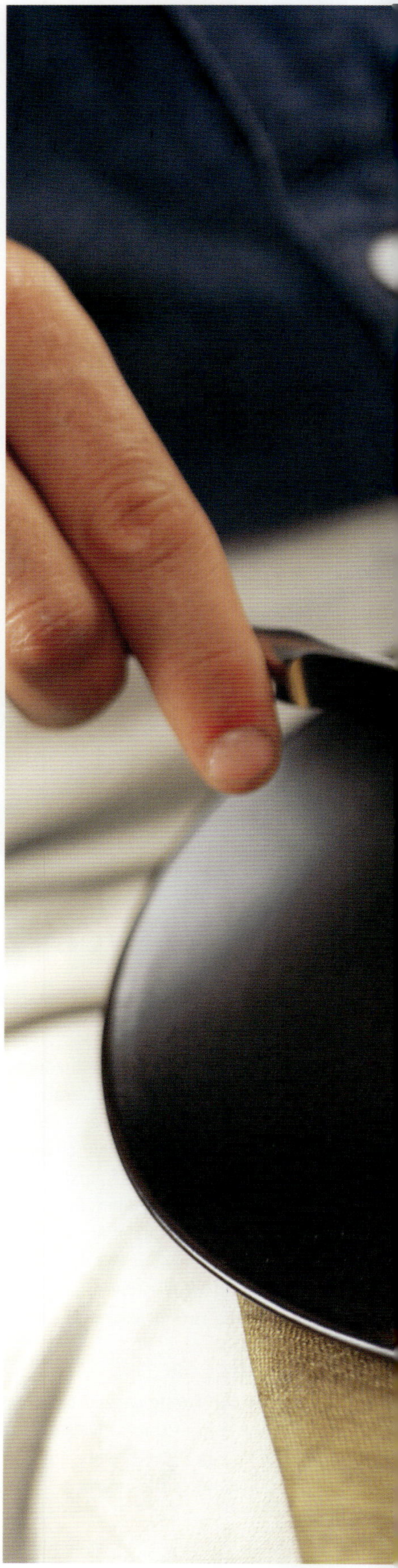

main meals

grilled beef fillet

with roast parsnip mash

preparation time 30 minutes (plus marinating time)
cooking time 1 hour

12 small beef eye fillet steaks (1.2kg)
1/3 cup (80ml) olive oil
1/4 cup (60ml) balsamic vinegar
1 tablespoon seeded mustard
8 large parsnips (1.8kg), chopped coarsely
1 1/2 cups (375ml) beef stock
1 tablespoon sugar
60g butter, chopped coarsely
2 cups (500ml) skim milk
500g spinach, trimmed
1/3 cup (85g) sour cream

1 Combine beef, oil, vinegar and mustard in large bowl. Cover; refrigerate 3 hours or overnight.

2 Heat oven to moderately hot.

3 Place parsnip, in single layer, on oiled oven trays. Bake, uncovered, in hot oven about 50 minutes or until tender.

4 Meanwhile, drain beef over medium saucepan; reserve marinade. Add stock and sugar to marinade; cook, stirring, over low heat until sugar dissolves. Bring to a boil; reduce heat, simmer, uncovered, about 10 minutes or until sauce reduces by a third.

5 Blend or process parsnip, butter and milk until pureed. Cover; keep warm.

6 Cook beef, in batches, on heated oiled grill plate (or grill or barbecue) until browned both sides and cooked as desired.

7 While beef stands, boil, steam or microwave spinach until just wilted. Meanwhile, whisk sour cream into sauce. Serve beef with parsnip mash and spinach; drizzle with sauce.

SERVES 6

per serving 39g fat; 2876kJ

tips Beef sirloin, scotch fillet or rump steak could be used instead of beef eye fillet.

The marinated beef can be frozen for up to six months.

serving suggestion Serve with steamed baby carrots and parsley.

cajun *fish steaks* with pumpkin and potato roast

preparation time 25 minutes ■ cooking time 50 minutes

You can use any firm white-fleshed fish fillet for this recipe.

- 1.5kg butternut pumpkin, chopped coarsely
- 1 large red onion (300g), chopped coarsely
- 3 large potatoes (900g), chopped coarsely
- 1/3 cup (80ml) olive oil
- 2 tablespoons onion powder
- 1 1/2 tablespoons garlic salt
- 2 teaspoons cracked black pepper
- 1 tablespoon mustard powder
- 1/2 teaspoon ground cayenne pepper
- 1 1/2 tablespoons sweet paprika
- 2 teaspoons fennel seeds
- 2 teaspoons celery seeds
- 6 swordfish steaks (1.2kg)
- 1 tablespoon sweet paprika, extra
- 1/4 cup firmly packed, coarsely chopped fresh coriander leaves

1. Preheat oven to very hot.
2. Combine pumpkin, onion, potato and 1 tablespoon of the oil in large baking dish. Roast, uncovered, in very hot oven about 40 minutes or until tender and browned lightly, stirring occasionally. Remove roasted vegetables from oven.
3. Combine onion powder, garlic salt, black pepper, mustard powder, cayenne pepper, paprika and seeds in medium bowl. Coat fish in spice mixture; cook on heated oiled grill plate (or grill or barbecue) until browned both sides and cooked as desired.
4. Heat remaining oil in small saucepan. Add extra paprika; cook, stirring, until fragrant. Strain through fine sieve over heatproof jug.
5. Serve fish with pumpkin and potato roast. Drizzle sweet paprika oil around edge of plate; sprinkle with coriander.

SERVES 6

per serving 22g fat; 2388kJ

tip Tiny school prawns, tossed in this spice mixture unshelled and deep-fried, are an authentic Cajun dish called "popcorn shrimp".

serving suggestion Serve with tall glasses of lime iced tea, and cabbage and snow pea sprout salad.

chicken dhania *masala*

preparation time 15 minutes ■ cooking time 30 minutes

Dhania is the Indian name for fresh coriander; this recipe calls for it to be processed into an aromatic paste (masala) to be cooked with the chicken.

1⅓ cups firmly packed fresh coriander leaves
⅔ cup firmly packed fresh mint leaves
1⅓ cups (330ml) water
2 teaspoons sesame oil
2 cloves garlic, quartered
2 tablespoons coarsely chopped fresh ginger
⅓ cup (80ml) white vinegar
2 teaspoons ground turmeric
2 teaspoons ground cumin
1 teaspoon ground cardamom
2 red thai chillies, seeded, quartered
1 teaspoon sea salt
2 tablespoons vegetable oil
12 chicken thigh cutlets (2kg)
2 large brown onions (400g), sliced thinly

1 Blend or process coriander, mint, the water, sesame oil, garlic, ginger, vinegar, spices, chilli and salt until masala mixture is well combined.

2 Heat half of the vegetable oil in large saucepan; cook chicken, in batches, until browned lightly and almost cooked through. Heat remaining vegetable oil in same pan; cook onion, stirring, until browned lightly. Add masala mixture; cook, stirring, about 5 minutes or until masala is cooked and fragrant. Add chicken; cook, covered, about 10 minutes or until chicken is cooked through.

SERVES 6

per serving 22.5g fat; 2096kJ

tip The masala paste can be made a day ahead and refrigerated, covered (it can also be frozen).

serving suggestion Serve potato and pea samosas before this curry.

ricotta and capsicum *ravioli* with rocket dressing

preparation time 40 minutes ■ cooking time 30 minutes

3 large red capsicums (1kg)
2 green onions, chopped finely
1 clove garlic, crushed
2½ cups (500g) ricotta cheese
72 wonton wrappers
300g baby rocket leaves
½ cup (125ml) olive oil
2 tablespoons lemon juice
2 tablespoons balsamic vinegar
2 teaspoons sugar
1 clove garlic, quartered, extra
¼ cup (20g) shaved parmesan cheese

1. Quarter capsicums; remove and discard seeds and membrane. Roast under grill or in very hot oven, skin-side up, until skin blisters and blackens. Cover capsicum quarters in plastic or paper for 5 minutes; peel away skin, then chop finely.
2. Combine capsicum, onion, garlic and ricotta in medium bowl.
3. Place 1 level tablespoon of the capsicum filling in the centre of each of 36 wonton wrappers. Brush edges lightly with a little water then top each with remaining wonton wrappers; press edges together to seal.
4. Reserve approximately a fifth of the rocket. Blend or process remaining rocket, oil, juice, vinegar, sugar and extra garlic until pureed. Strain into medium jug; discard pulp.
5. Cook ravioli, in batches, in large saucepan of boiling water, uncovered, until tender; drain. Serve ravioli drizzled with rocket dressing; top with reserved rocket and parmesan.

SERVES 6

per serving 30.9g fat; 1913kJ

tip Make the ravioli a day ahead; place on a tray and refrigerate, covered, until just before you want to cook them.

If you need to stack the ravioli as you make them (to save on space), top each layer with plastic wrap first – so the ravioli don't stick together.

serving suggestion
Serve with a white-bean and tomato salad in a garlic lemon dressing.

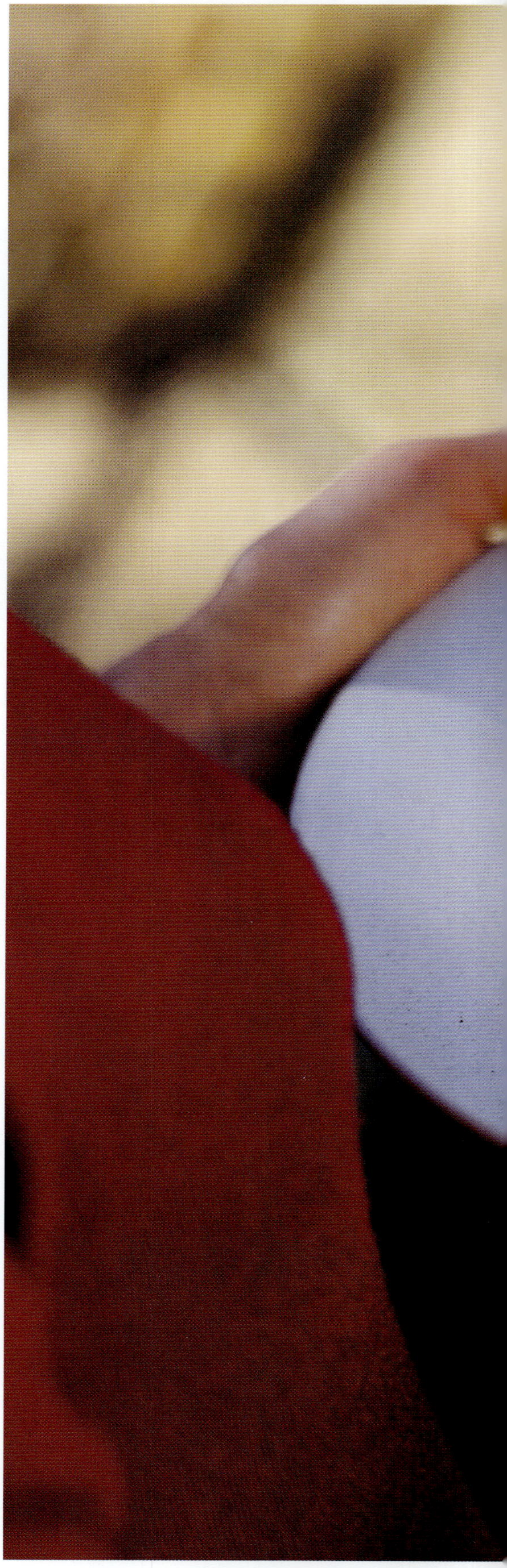

moroccan *lamb shanks*
with polenta and white beans

preparation time 25 minutes (plus soaking time) ■ cooking time 2 hours

$1\frac{1}{2}$ cups (300g) dried haricot beans
12 french-trimmed lamb shanks (approximately 2.6kg)
$\frac{1}{4}$ cup (35g) plain flour
1 tablespoon olive oil
2 medium red onions (340g), chopped finely
2 cloves garlic, crushed
2 teaspoons ground cumin
$\frac{1}{2}$ teaspoon ground cardamom
$\frac{1}{2}$ teaspoon ground ginger
2 teaspoons finely grated lemon rind
$\frac{1}{3}$ cup (80ml) lemon juice
2 x 400g cans tomatoes
$2\frac{1}{2}$ cups (625ml) beef stock
$\frac{1}{4}$ cup (70g) tomato paste
3 cups (750ml) water
3 cups (750ml) milk
2 cups (340g) polenta
2 teaspoons finely grated lemon rind, extra
$\frac{1}{4}$ cup loosely packed, finely chopped fresh flat-leaf parsley
$\frac{1}{4}$ cup loosely packed, finely chopped fresh coriander leaves

1. Cover beans with cold water in large bowl. Soak overnight; drain.
2. Coat lamb in flour; shake off excess. Heat oil in large saucepan; cook lamb, in batches, until browned all over. Add onion and garlic; cook, stirring, until onion is soft. Add spices to pan; cook, stirring, about 2 minutes or until fragrant.
3. Stir in beans, rind, juice, undrained crushed tomatoes, stock and paste; bring to a boil. Reduce heat; simmer, covered, 40 minutes. Uncover; simmer about 50 minutes or until both lamb and beans are tender.
4. Heat the water and milk in large saucepan (do not boil). Add polenta; cook, stirring, about 5 minutes or until liquid is absorbed and polenta softens.
5. Serve lamb mixture on polenta, sprinkled with combined extra rind, parsley and coriander.

SERVES 6

per serving 15.1g fat; 3114kJ

tips You can use any dried bean (navy, cannellini, great northern or even chickpeas) in this recipe.

The lamb and bean mixture is especially good if made the day before serving and refrigerated, covered (it's also suitable to freeze).

serving suggestion Start the meal with a Moroccan-style orange and radish salad, then follow with this main course.

mixed vegetable and lentil *curry*

preparation time 15 minutes ■ cooking time 30 minutes

You need a whole cauliflower weighing about 700g for this recipe.

- 2 tablespoons peanut oil
- 2 large brown onions (400g), chopped coarsely
- 2 cloves garlic, crushed
- 1 tablespoon grated fresh ginger
- 2 tablespoons red curry paste
- 1.5 litres (6 cups) vegetable stock
- 2 cups (400g) red lentils
- 4 medium carrots (480g), chopped coarsely
- 250g baby green beans
- 500g cauliflower florets
- 1 cup (250ml) coconut milk
- 1/4 cup coarsely chopped fresh coriander leaves

1. Heat oil in large saucepan; cook onion, stirring, about 5 minutes or until very soft. Add garlic, ginger and paste; cook, stirring, until fragrant.
2. Add stock and lentils; bring to a boil. Reduce heat; simmer, uncovered, 5 minutes. Add carrot, beans and cauliflower; simmer, uncovered, about 10 minutes or until vegetables are tender.
3. Add coconut milk and coriander; cook, stirring, until heated through.

SERVES 6

per serving 20g fat; 1847kJ

tips You can use your favourite curry paste in this recipe.

Curry can be made a day ahead and refrigerated, covered.

If using packaged stock you can use half stock and half water, as the flavour is very concentrated.

serving suggestion Serve with steamed basmati rice, cucumber raita and chilli-flavoured pappadums.

barbecued *veal chops* with polenta

preparation time 20 minutes (plus refrigeration time) ■ cooking time 1 hour

3 cups (750ml) water
1/2 cup (125ml) milk
1 1/2 cups (255g) polenta
1 teaspoon sea salt
1 teaspoon cracked black pepper
6 large (1.5kg) tomatoes, quartered
1 tablespoon balsamic vinegar
6 veal loin chops (1kg)
150g baby spinach leaves

RED WINE SAUCE

20g butter
1 small brown onion (80g), chopped finely
1 clove garlic, crushed
1 tablespoon plain flour
1 1/2 cups (375ml) beef stock
1/2 cup (125ml) dry red wine
1 tablespoon brown sugar
1 tablespoon tomato paste

1. Preheat oven to hot. Oil 19cm x 29cm rectangular slice pan.
2. Heat the water and milk in large saucepan (do not boil). Add polenta; cook, stirring, about 5 minutes or until liquid is absorbed and polenta thickens. Stir in salt and pepper. Spoon polenta into prepared pan; press firmly to ensure even thickness. When cool, cover; refrigerate about 2 hours or until firm.
3. Meanwhile, combine tomato and vinegar in baking dish; roast, uncovered, in hot oven about 35 minutes or until soft. Cover; keep warm.
4. Turn polenta onto board; trim edges. Cut into six squares; cut each square in half diagonally. Cook polenta on heated oiled grill plate (or grill or barbecue) until browned both sides and heated through. Cover; keep warm.
5. Cook veal on heated oiled grill plate (or grill or barbecue) until browned both sides and cooked as desired. Serve veal with tomato, polenta and spinach, drizzled with red wine sauce.

red wine sauce Melt butter in medium saucepan; cook onion and garlic, stirring, until onion is soft. Stir in flour; cook, stirring, until mixture bubbles. Add stock, wine, sugar and paste; cook, stirring, about 5 minutes or until mixture thickens. Strain into small jug.

SERVES 6

per serving 7.3g fat; 1597kJ

tip While we used a merlot, similar in flavour to a cabernet sauvignon but slightly softer and more mellow, you can use any dry red wine you like; it's a nice idea to serve the same wine variety with this dish.

serving suggestion Serve with a simply dressed green leaf salad.

seared salmon

with pistachio-coriander pesto and pumpkin couscous

preparation time 25 minutes ■ cooking time 25 minutes

500g butternut pumpkin, chopped finely
2 teaspoons ground coriander
2 teaspoons ground cumin
1/4 cup (60ml) olive oil
1/4 cup (35g) shelled pistachios, toasted
1/4 cup (40g) pine nuts, toasted
1 cup firmly packed fresh coriander leaves
1 tablespoon lemon juice
2 cloves garlic, quartered
6 small salmon fillets (approximately 1kg)
2 cups (400g) couscous
20g butter, chopped coarsely
2 cups (500ml) boiling water
1 small red onion (100g), chopped finely

1. Preheat oven to hot.
2. Combine pumpkin and spices in large baking dish; drizzle with 1 tablespoon of the olive oil. Bake, uncovered, in hot oven about 25 minutes or until browned and tender, turning pumpkin occasionally to cook evenly.
3. Meanwhile, blend or process nuts, coriander, juice, garlic and remaining oil until mixture forms a paste.
4. Cook salmon on heated oiled grill plate (or grill or barbecue) until browned both sides and cooked as desired.
5. Combine couscous and butter with the water in large heatproof bowl. Cover; stand about 5 minutes or until water is absorbed, fluffing couscous with fork constantly to separate grains. Stir in spiced pumpkin and onion.
6. Serve salmon on couscous, topped with pesto.

SERVES 6

per serving 31.4g fat; 2681kJ

tips You can use any kind of nuts in this pesto, and rocket can be substituted for the coriander.

Pesto can be made up to two days ahead and refrigerated, covered, until just before serving.

serving suggestion Serve with a simple lettuce and tomato salad.

lemon chicken
with fresh egg noodles

preparation time 20 minutes
cooking time 20 minutes (plus standing time)

1kg chicken breast fillets
500g fresh asparagus
2 medium lemons (280g)
2 tablespoons vegetable oil
500g fresh egg noodles
4 cloves garlic, crushed
1 tablespoon grated fresh ginger
4 green onions, sliced thickly
1 cup (250ml) chicken stock
2 teaspoons fish sauce
1/4 cup (60ml) lemon juice
10 basil leaves, torn

1. Cut chicken into 3cm pieces. Slice asparagus diagonally into 3cm lengths. Halve lemons lengthways; slice thinly.
2. Heat half of the oil in wok or large frying pan; stir-fry chicken, in batches, until browned lightly. Add lemon; stir-fry about 2 minutes or until browned. Add to chicken.
3. Place noodles in large heatproof bowl; cover with boiling water. Stand until just tender; drain.
4. Meanwhile, heat remaining oil in same wok; stir-fry garlic, ginger, asparagus and onion about 2 minutes or until vegetables are just soft.
5. Return chicken, noodles and lemon to wok with combined stock, sauce and juice; stir-fry, tossing, until hot. Remove from heat, stir in basil.

SERVES 8

per serving 8.5g fat; 1243kJ

tip Chicken thigh fillets can be used in this recipe.

serving suggestion Serve with stir-fried baby bok choy with ginger and garlic.

grilled *scotch fillet steaks*

with caramelised onion and garlic mushrooms

preparation time 25 minutes (plus marinating time) ■ cooking time 45 minutes

- 6 beef scotch fillet steaks (approximately 1.25kg)
- 1/2 cup (125ml) dry red wine
- 2 tablespoons finely chopped fresh basil leaves
- 2 cloves garlic, crushed
- 6 large flat mushrooms (840g)
- 2 tablespoons olive oil
- 1 clove garlic, crushed, extra
- 1 teaspoon lemon pepper
- 20g butter
- 6 medium red onions (1kg), sliced thinly
- 1/3 cup (75g) firmly packed brown sugar
- 1/4 cup (60ml) red wine vinegar

1. Combine beef, wine, basil and garlic in large bowl. Cover; refrigerate 3 hours or overnight.
2. Preheat oven to hot.
3. Place mushrooms in large shallow baking dish. Drizzle with oil; sprinkle with extra garlic and lemon pepper. Bake, uncovered, in hot oven about 25 minutes or until tender.
4. Meanwhile, melt butter in large frying pan; cook onion, stirring, until soft and browned lightly. Stir in sugar and vinegar; cook, stirring constantly, about 20 minutes or until onion is well browned and mixture thickened.
5. Drain beef; discard marinade. Cook beef, in batches, on heated oiled grill plate (or grill or barbecue) until browned both sides and cooked as desired.
6. Top each steak with a mushroom and a little caramelised onion.

SERVES 6

per serving 22.7g fat; 2155kJ

tips Balsamic vinegar can be substituted for red wine vinegar.

You can freeze the marinated beef and cook at a later date, if you prefer. Place marinated beef in a storage container or freezer bag and freeze for up to six months.

serving suggestion Serve with creamy mashed potatoes.

prawn and asparagus *risotto*

preparation time 30 minutes ■ cooking time 50 minutes

32 medium uncooked prawns (approximately 1kg)
500g fresh asparagus
1.5 litres (6 cups) chicken stock
1½ cups (375ml) dry white wine
30g butter
1 large brown onion (200g), chopped finely
2 cloves garlic, crushed
3 cups (600g) arborio rice
2 medium tomatoes (380g), seeded, chopped finely
⅓ cup loosely packed, coarsely chopped fresh flat-leaf parsley
½ teaspoon cracked black pepper

1. Shell and devein prawns, leaving tails intact. Slice asparagus diagonally into 3cm lengths.
2. Combine stock and wine in large saucepan. Bring to a boil; cover. Reduce heat; simmer to keep hot.
3. Melt butter in large saucepan; cook onion and garlic, stirring, until onion is soft. Add rice; stir to coat in butter mixture. Stir in 1 cup of the hot stock mixture; cook, stirring, over low heat until liquid is absorbed. Continue adding stock mixture, in 1-cup batches, stirring, until liquid is absorbed after each addition. Total cooking time should be about 35 minutes or until rice is just tender.
4. Add prawns, asparagus, tomato, parsley and pepper; cook, stirring, until prawns are just changed in colour and asparagus is tender.

SERVES 6

per serving 5.6g fat; 2444kJ

tip If arborio rice is unavailable, use the shortest, most round-grain white rice you can find. Long-grained rice will always remain as individual grains, never absorbing enough liquid to achieve the proper soupy-soft texture of a perfect risotto.

serving suggestion Serve with a warm loaf of ciabatta and a mixed green salad.

pan-fried *blue-eye cutlets*

with potato crisps and gingered carrots

preparation time 25 minutes ■ cooking time 40 minutes

We used pontiac potatoes here because they are excellent for baking. You can use any firm white-fleshed fish for this recipe. Green ginger wine is an alcoholic beverage with the taste of fresh ginger. In cooking, you can substitute it with a dry (white) vermouth, if you prefer.

6 medium potatoes (1.2kg)
cooking-oil spray
4 large carrots (720g)
10cm piece ginger
2 bunches chives
2 tablespoons olive oil
2 cloves garlic, crushed
6 blue-eye cutlets (1.5kg)
1/3 cup (50g) plain flour
3/4 cup (180ml) lemon juice
1/4 cup (60ml) green ginger wine
2 1/2 cups (625ml) fish stock

1 Preheat oven to hot.

2 Cut potatoes into 5mm-thick slices. Place, in single layer, on oiled oven trays; coat with cooking-oil spray. Roast, uncovered, in hot oven about 40 minutes or until browned lightly.

3 Meanwhile, cut carrots and ginger into 2mm-wide lengths, then into thin strips. Cut chives in half.

4 Heat half of the oil in large frying pan; cook carrot, ginger and garlic, in batches, stirring, about 2 minutes or until carrot is just tender. Stir chives into carrot mixture; cover to keep warm.

5 Coat fish in flour; shake off excess. Heat remaining oil in same pan; cook fish, in batches, until browned lightly and cooked as desired. Drain oil from pan; add juice, wine and stock. Bring to a boil; simmer, uncovered, about 10 minutes or until sauce thickens.

6 Divide potato slices among serving plates. Top with gingered carrots then fish; drizzle with sauce.

SERVES 6

per serving 14.1g fat; 2263kJ

tip Tuna and swordfish are both excellent substitutes for blue-eye.

serving suggestion Serve with warmed bread rolls and olives.

gremolata-crumbed roast

leg of lamb

preparation time 15 minutes (plus marinating time)
cooking time 1 hour 40 minutes

1.7kg leg of lamb
1/4 cup (60ml) lemon juice
4 cloves garlic, crushed
5 large potatoes (1.5kg)
1 medium brown onion (150g), chopped finely
2 trimmed sticks celery (150g), chopped finely
2 tablespoons plain flour
1/2 cup (125ml) dry red wine
2 cups (500ml) beef stock
2 sprigs fresh rosemary
1 tablespoon finely chopped fresh flat-leaf parsley

GREMOLATA

1/2 cup loosely packed, finely chopped fresh flat-leaf parsley
1 tablespoon finely grated lemon rind
2 cloves garlic, crushed
1/2 cup (35g) stale breadcrumbs
1 tablespoon olive oil

1. Combine lamb with juice and half of the garlic in large bowl. Cover; refrigerate 3 hours or overnight, turning lamb occasionally in marinade.
2. Preheat oven to moderate. Cut each potato into eight wedges.
3. Place undrained lamb and potato in large flameproof baking dish; roast, uncovered, in moderate oven 1 hour.
4. Press gremolata mixture onto lamb; roast, uncovered, in moderate oven about 30 minutes or until lamb is cooked as desired.
5. Remove lamb and potato from baking dish. Cover; keep warm. Cook onion, celery and remaining garlic in baking dish, stirring, until vegetables are soft. Stir in flour; cook, stirring, about 1 minute or until bubbling. Gradually stir in wine and stock, add rosemary; cook, stirring, until gravy thickens. Strain gravy into medium jug.
6. Serve lamb and potato wedges with gravy; sprinkle with parsley.

gremolata Combine ingredients in small bowl.

SERVES 6

per serve 15.1g fat; 2208kJ

serving suggestion Serve with garlicky green beans and carrots.

garlic *chicken* with warm roasted-tomato tabbouleh

preparation time 40 minutes (plus marinating time) ■ cooking time 35 minutes (plus standing time)

6 single chicken breast fillets (1kg)
2 cloves garlic, crushed
2 tablespoons olive oil
2 teaspoons finely grated lemon rind
1 teaspoon lemon pepper
1/2 teaspoon sweet paprika
500g cherry tomatoes
1/3 cup (55g) burghul
5 cups firmly packed fresh flat-leaf parsley, chopped coarsely
1 cup firmly packed fresh mint leaves, chopped coarsely
4 green onions, chopped finely
1 small red onion (100g), chopped finely
2 tablespoons olive oil, extra
1/4 cup (60ml) lemon juice

1 Combine chicken, garlic, half of the oil, rind, lemon pepper and paprika in large bowl. Cover; refrigerate 3 hours or overnight.

2 Preheat oven to hot.

3 Combine tomatoes and remaining oil in large baking dish. Roast in hot oven, uncovered, about 25 minutes or until browned lightly and just softened.

4 Meanwhile, cover burghul with cold water in medium bowl; stand 20 minutes. Drain burghul, squeezing with hands to remove as much water as possible. Combine burghul with parsley, mint, onions, extra oil, juice and hot tomatoes in large bowl.

5 Drain chicken; discard marinade. Cook chicken, in batches, on heated oiled grill plate (or grill or barbecue) until browned both sides and cooked through.

6 Serve chicken with warm roasted-tomato tabbouleh.

SERVES 6

per serving 17g fat; 1472kJ

tips "Chop" parsley and mint leaves together in a large bowl using scissors.

You can freeze the marinated chicken and cook at a later date, if you prefer. Place chicken, in the marinade, in a storage container or freezer bag; seal tightly and freeze for up to six months.

serving suggestion Serve with grilled lemons and toasted pide.

roast pork with chilli cabbage salad

preparation time 25 minutes (plus marinating time) ■ cooking time 1 hour 45 minutes

- 12-cutlet rack of pork (approximately 2.5kg)
- 1/2 cup (125ml) lime juice
- 1/3 cup (80ml) olive oil
- 3 cloves garlic, crushed
- 2 tablespoons sherry vinegar
- 2 teaspoons sugar
- 1 tablespoon cumin seeds, toasted
- 2 teaspoons salt
- 2 cups (500ml) vegetable stock
- 1kg savoy cabbage, shredded finely
- 5 large dill pickles, drained, chopped finely
- 1/4 cup (65g) finely chopped drained jalapeño chillies
- 1/4 cup firmly packed, finely chopped fresh mint leaves
- 4 green onions, chopped finely

1. Combine pork, juice, oil, garlic, vinegar, sugar and seeds in large baking dish. Cover; refrigerate 3 hours or overnight.
2. Preheat oven to hot.
3. Drain pork over large saucepan; reserve marinade. Place pork upright on rack in large baking dish; rub salt into rind. Roast, uncovered, in hot oven 30 minutes. Reduce oven temperature to moderate; roast, uncovered, about 1 hour or until pork is tender. Cover loosely with foil; allow to stand while preparing salad.
4. Meanwhile, add stock to reserved marinade; bring to a boil. Reduce heat; simmer, uncovered, about 10 minutes or until sauce reduces by about a third.
5. Toss cabbage in large bowl with pickle, chilli, mint and onion.
6. Cut rack into six serving portions. Serve pork cutlets on salad; drizzle with sauce.

SERVES 6

per serving 77.2g fat; 4400kJ

tips You can buy individual pork chops, if you wish, then grill or barbecue them after marinating.

Jalapeño chillies, sold canned or bottled in brine, are available whole or already sliced. If you buy the latter, you may wish to chop them even more finely before adding to the cabbage salad.

After marinating, the pork is suitable to freeze for up to six months.

serving suggestion Serve with a kumara and potato mash.

on the side

vine-ripened tomatoes

and goat cheese in walnut dressing

preparation time 15 minutes

8 medium vine-ripened tomatoes (1.5kg), sliced thickly
150g goat cheese, sliced thickly
1/4 cup (25g) walnuts, toasted, chopped coarsely
1/4 cup (60ml) olive oil
1 clove garlic, crushed
1 1/2 tablespoons raspberry vinegar
2 teaspoons dijon mustard
2 teaspoons coarsely chopped fresh thyme
2 teaspoons sugar

1 Place one slice of tomato on each serving plate; top with a slice of cheese. Repeat, sprinkling nuts and combined remaining ingredients between layers.

SERVES 6

per serving 18.5g fat; 938kJ

tips Hazelnuts can be substituted for walnuts in this recipe, and, if you have hazelnut or walnut oil on hand, use one of these, rather than the olive oil.

Sample a few different goat cheeses before you decide on one: they vary greatly in texture and taste.

serving suggestion Serve this salad with a simple chicken or fish main course.

lentil salad with sesame seeds and coriander

preparation time 15 minutes ■ cooking time 20 minutes

- ½ cup (100g) red lentils
- ½ cup (100g) brown lentils
- 2 tablespoons toasted sesame seeds
- 1 large yellow capsicum (350g), chopped finely
- 1 small red onion (100g), chopped finely
- ½ cup loosely packed fresh coriander leaves
- 50g baby spinach leaves, shredded finely
- ¼ cup (60ml) olive oil
- 2 tablespoons lemon juice
- 1 teaspoon ground cumin

1 Cook lentils, separately, uncovered, in small saucepans of boiling water until just tender; drain.

2 Combine lentils in large bowl with seeds, capsicum, onion, coriander and spinach; toss gently with combined remaining ingredients.

SERVES 4

per serving 19.1g fat; 1341kJ

tip Any leftover salad, drained and rolled in a piece of pitta or naan, will make a healthy sandwich the following day.

serving suggestion Serve with tandoori chicken and steamed basmati rice.

warm cherry- and teardrop-
tomato salad

preparation time 15 minutes ■ cooking time 15 minutes

Yellow teardrop tomatoes are slightly smaller and more acidic than cherry tomatoes, and are more pear-shaped than round.

1kg cherry tomatoes, halved
500g yellow teardrop tomatoes, halved
10 green onions
2 cloves garlic, crushed
2 tablespoons balsamic vinegar
2 tablespoons olive oil
2 tablespoons water
2 teaspoons sugar
1 teaspoon salt
1 cup (180g) niçoise olives, seeded
1 tablespoon finely shredded fresh mint leaves

1 Cook tomatoes, in batches, in lightly oiled non-stick frying pan until just softened. Remove from pan; place in large bowl.

2 Cut onions into 8cm lengths. Cook, in same pan, until soft; combine with tomatoes.

3 Cook garlic, vinegar, oil, the water, sugar and salt in same pan, stirring, about 3 minutes or until dressing thickens slightly.

4 Pour hot dressing over tomato mixture. Add olives and mint; toss gently to combine.

SERVES 6

per serving 20.6g fat; 1073kJ

tip Seeded kalamata olives can be substituted for the niçoise olives.

serving suggestion This salad can be served as an entree or with a simple fish dish.

Opposite (left to right):
warm cherry- and teardrop-tomato salad;
mesclun with pine nuts in lime vinaigrette;
lentil salad with sesame seeds and coriander

mesclun with pine nuts in lime vinaigrette

preparation time 12 minutes

Mesclun is a mixture of assorted young lettuce and other green leaves.

4 green onions
400g mesclun
1/4 cup (40g) pine nuts, toasted

LIME VINAIGRETTE

1/4 cup (60ml) lime juice
1/4 cup (60ml) peanut oil
2 cloves garlic, crushed
1 teaspoon sugar

1 Cut onions into 10cm lengths; slice finely. Place onion in bowl of iced water; stand about 10 minutes or until onion curls.

2 Place drained onion in large bowl with mesclun and nuts; toss gently with lime vinaigrette.

lime vinaigrette Combine ingredients in screw-top jar; shake well.

SERVES 8

per serving 10.8g fat; 460kJ

tip Trimmed onions can be placed in a small bowl of water and refrigerated, covered, overnight.

serving suggestion An accompaniment of grilled mixed mushrooms turns this simple salad into a light main meal.

asian greens in oyster sauce

preparation time 10 minutes ■ cooking time 10 minutes

1 cup (250ml) chicken stock
1/3 cup (80ml) oyster sauce
2 teaspoons sesame oil
2kg baby bok choy, trimmed
1kg choy sum, trimmed

1 Combine stock, sauce and oil in wok or large frying pan; bring mixture to a boil.

2 Add bok choy; cook, stirring, about 3 minutes or until bok choy is slightly wilted.

3 Stir in choy sum; cook, covered, about 5 minutes or until both greens are tender and just wilted.

SERVES 6

per serving 1.9g fat; 211kJ

tip Use any leafy green Asian vegetables you like in this recipe but be certain that you prepare the recipe just before serving.

serving suggestion Serve with Chinese barbecued pork or duck and steamed rice.

potato salad with herb vinaigrette

preparation time 15 minutes ■ cooking time 15 minutes

2kg tiny new potatoes, halved
1/3 cup firmly packed, finely chopped fresh mint leaves
1/3 cup firmly packed, finely chopped fresh flat-leaf parsley
1/3 cup (80ml) red wine vinegar
1/4 cup (60ml) olive oil
2 tablespoons brown sugar

1 Boil, steam or microwave potato until tender. Drain; keep warm.

2 Combine remaining ingredients in large bowl.

3 Gently toss potato with vinaigrette mixture until combined.

SERVES 8

per serving 7.4g fat; 1002kJ

tip Make the vinaigrette a day ahead to allow the flavours to blend, and refrigerate, covered, overnight.

serving suggestion Serve with barbecued lamb kofta or beef kebabs.

roast potatoes with mustard and dill pickle sauce

preparation time 10 minutes ■ cooking time 1 hour 30 minutes

Kipflers, small, irregularly shaped, nutty-tasting potatoes, are particularly well-disposed towards being oven-roasted and used in salads.

1kg kipfler potatoes
5 small red onions (500g), quartered
1 tablespoon sea salt
2 cloves garlic, crushed
$^1/_2$ cup (125ml) olive oil
1 tablespoon dijon mustard
1 tablespoon seeded mustard
2 tablespoons balsamic vinegar
400g bottled small dill pickles, drained, halved

1 Preheat oven to moderately hot.

2 Combine potatoes, onion, salt, garlic and half of the oil in large baking dish; toss gently to combine. Roast potato mixture, uncovered, in moderately hot oven about $1^1/_2$ hours or until potatoes are tender, stirring halfway during cooking.

3 Combine remaining oil in large bowl with remaining ingredients. Just before serving, add potato mixture to bowl; toss to combine.

SERVES 6

per serving 20.3g fat; 1329kJ

tip Any good roasting potatoes (pontiac, sebago, desiree or king edward can be substituted for the kipflers in this recipe)

serving suggestion Serve with grilled tuna or salmon.

zucchini ribbon salad with spearmint and almonds

preparation time 20 minutes

There are many varieties of mint, but one of the most common is the grey-green spearmint with its mild flavour and delicate aroma. It grows wild in many of our gardens during summer but your greengrocer should be able to obtain it for you all year long.

4 medium green zucchini (480g)
4 medium yellow zucchini (480g)
1/2 cup (80g) blanched almonds, toasted
2 large red capsicums (700g), sliced thinly
1/3 cup finely chopped fresh spearmint leaves

RASPBERRY VINAIGRETTE

1/2 cup (125ml) olive oil
1 tablespoon lemon juice
1 teaspoon finely grated lemon rind
2 tablespoons raspberry vinegar

1 Using vegetable peeler, cut zucchini into thin ribbons.

2 Place zucchini in large bowl with almonds, capsicum and mint; toss gently with raspberry vinaigrette.

raspberry vinaigrette Combine ingredients in screw-top jar; shake well and toss through salad.

SERVES 6

per serving 27.9g fat; 1264kJ

tip Select mint leaves that are evenly coloured and have no brown tinge around the edges. A bunch of mint can be kept, stems in a jar of water and leaves covered with a plastic bag, in the refrigerator, up to 5 days.

serving suggestion Serve with a whole poached fish.

creamed spinach (back); kumara mash (front)

creamed spinach

preparation time 25 minutes
cooking time 15 minutes
(plus cooling time)

- 1.25kg spinach, trimmed
- 40g butter
- 1 medium brown onion (150g), chopped coarsely
- 2 cloves garlic, quartered
- 1/4 teaspoon ground nutmeg
- 1/3 cup (80ml) dry white wine
- 1/2 cup (125ml) cream
- 1/2 cup (125ml) chicken stock

1. Boil, steam or microwave spinach, until just wilted; drain. Cool 5 minutes; squeeze out as much excess liquid as possible.
2. Melt butter in large saucepan; cook onion and garlic, stirring, until onion is soft. Stir in nutmeg; cook, stirring, about 1 minute or until fragrant.
3. Add wine; bring to a boil. Simmer, uncovered, until reduced by half. Stir in spinach, cream and stock; cook, stirring, about 2 minutes or until hot.
4. Blend or process spinach mixture until pureed. Return to same pan; reheat, stirring, until hot.

SERVES 6

per serving 14.8g fat; 706kJ

tip To extract as much water as possible from the spinach, roll it in a tea-towel or absorbent paper, squeezing it with your hands. Any residual water in the spinach will give you a watery rather than creamy result.

serving suggestion Perfect with kumara mash and roast chicken.

kumara mash

preparation time 10 minutes ■ cooking time 1 hour

- 4 large kumara (2kg), chopped coarsely
- 2 tablespoons olive oil
- 1 cup (250ml) buttermilk
- 20g butter

1. Preheat oven to moderately hot.
2. Combine kumara in large baking dish with oil; roast, uncovered, in moderately hot oven about 1 hour or until kumara is tender.
3. Blend or process kumara with remaining ingredients until pureed. Return to same pan; reheat, stirring, until hot.

SERVES 8

per serving 7.7g fat; 910kJ

tips Make the mash just before serving.

Add a little lemon juice or a few tablespoons of a freshly chopped herb such as thyme, dill or even flat-leaf parsley.

serving suggestion Serve with grilled rib steaks and slow-roasted tomatoes.

broad bean salad with anchovy dressing

preparation time 30 minutes ■ cooking time 10 minutes

1kg frozen broad beans, thawed
8 anchovy fillets, drained
1/3 cup (80ml) lemon juice
1/3 cup (80ml) olive oil
2 cloves garlic, quartered
2 teaspoons drained bottled capers
1 bunch fresh chives
1 medium red onion (170g), chopped finely

1 Boil, steam or microwave beans until just tender; drain. Rinse immediately under cold water to halt cooking process; drain. Peel away and discard outer beige shell.

2 Blend or process anchovies, juice, oil, garlic and capers until pureed.

3 Cut chives into 2cm lengths.

4 Combine beans, anchovy mixture, chives and onion in large bowl; toss gently to combine.

SERVES 6

per serving 16.7g fat; 948kJ

tip If fresh broad beans are in season, use them rather than the frozen variety. You will need to buy 1.5kg fresh broad beans in their pods; shell before cooking until just tender.

serving suggestion Serve with a caramelised onion tart.

fresh *asparagus* topped with garlic breadcrumbs and chopped eggs

preparation time 10 minutes ■ cooking time 10 minutes

This is our version of the classic French polonaise, vegetables served with grated hard-boiled eggs and breadcrumbs scattered over the top.

80g butter
2 tablespoons honey
2 cloves garlic, crushed
1 cup (70g) stale breadcrumbs
1kg fresh asparagus, trimmed
2 hard-boiled eggs, chopped finely
1/3 cup coarsely chopped flat-leaf parsley

1 Melt half of the butter and half of the honey in large frying pan. Add garlic and breadcrumbs; cook, stirring, until breadcrumbs are browned and crisp.

2 Boil, steam or microwave asparagus until just tender; drain.

3 Serve asparagus scattered with breadcrumb mixture, egg and parsley; drizzle with combined remaining melted butter and honey.

SERVES 8

per serving 9.9g fat; 621kJ

tip This recipe is best made just before serving, so breadcrumbs stay crisp.

One of the easiest ways to dice an egg is to use an egg slice. After slicing in one direction, hold egg and turn at 90 degree angle; slice a second time, cutting egg into cubes. If you don't have an egg slice, you can use a grater.

serving suggestion Serve with grilled lamb cutlets and lemon wedges.

Grating hard-boiled eggs

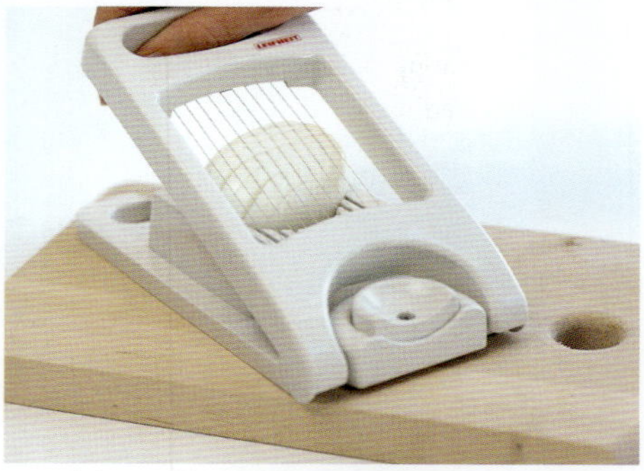

Second slicing of hard-boiled egg using egg slice

chickpea salad

preparation time 20 minutes (plus soaking time) ■ cooking time 50 minutes

1½ cups (300g) dried chickpeas
250g cherry tomatoes, halved
1 large green cucumber (400g), seeded, chopped coarsely
2 trimmed celery sticks (150g), chopped coarsely
1 medium red onion (170g), chopped finely
¼ cup firmly packed, finely chopped fresh mint leaves
½ teaspoon sea salt
¼ cup (60ml) lime juice
¼ cup (60ml) olive oil
2 teaspoons dijon mustard
¼ teaspoon sugar
2 cloves garlic, crushed

1 Place chickpeas in large bowl; cover with water. Soak overnight; drain.

2 Cook chickpeas in large saucepan of boiling water, uncovered, about 50 minutes or until tender; drain. Rinse under cold water; drain.

3 Combine chickpeas in large bowl with tomato, cucumber, celery, onion, mint and salt; toss gently with combined remaining ingredients.

SERVES 8

per serving 9.5g fat; 776kJ

tip You can use canned rather than the dried chickpeas called for here. Rinse two 400g cans of chickpeas well under cold water; allow to drain thoroughly before combining with other ingredients. This recipe can be made a day ahead and refrigerated, covered, overnight.

serving suggestion Serve with grilled marinated lamb skewers.

cabbage and *snow pea sprout* salad

preparation time 20 minutes

- 1 small savoy cabbage (1.2kg), shredded finely
- 1 medium yellow capsicum (200g), sliced thinly
- 160g snow pea sprouts
- 4 green onions, chopped finely
- 1/3 cup (80ml) lemon juice
- 1/4 cup (60ml) peanut oil
- 1 1/2 teaspoons sugar
- 1 tablespoon seeded mustard

1 Combine cabbage, capsicum, sprouts and onion in large bowl; toss gently with combined remaining ingredients.

SERVES 8

per serving 7.3g fat; 377kJ

tip Use red cabbage for a spectacularly coloured salad, and do not toss in the dressing until just before serving.

serving suggestion This salad goes really well with barbecued pork spareribs and cornmeal muffins.

mixed greens, *cucumber* and mint salad

preparation time 15 minutes

Vietnamese mint, also known as cambodian mint and laksa leaf, is a pungent, narrow-leafed herb frequently used in many South-East Asian soups and salads.

4 lebanese cucumbers (520g)
2 medium butter lettuce, trimmed
2 medium radicchio (400g), trimmed
1/2 cup loosely packed fresh vietnamese mint leaves
1 red banana chilli, seeded, chopped finely
1 tablespoon finely sliced fresh lemon grass
1/2 cup (125ml) peanut oil
3 teaspoons sesame oil
1 tablespoon raw sugar
2 teaspoons finely grated lime rind
1/4 cup (60ml) lime juice

1 Cut cucumbers diagonally into thin slices.

2 Combine cucumber, lettuces and mint in large bowl; gently toss with combined remaining ingredients.

SERVES 8

per serving 17g fat; 749kJ

tips Fresh mint can be substituted for vietnamese mint in this recipe.

Banana chilli is a sweet-flavoured chilli with a long, tapering shape. If unavailable, substitute with red capsicum.

Prepare salad just before serving.

Serving suggestion Serve with a platter of barbecued prawns.

desserts

poached pears in raspberry and vanilla-bean syrup

preparation time 15 minutes (plus refrigeration time)
cooking time 30 minutes (plus cooling time)

A vanilla bean is the long, dried pod from the vanilla orchid which grows in Mexico, Madagascar and Tahiti. Splitting a bean open releases thousands of tiny black seeds which are used directly in sauces, ice-cream mixtures and syrups to impart their aromatic sweetness to the flavour of the finished dish.

6 medium corella pears (1kg)
1 cup (220g) sugar
2 cups (500ml) water
1 vanilla bean
150g fresh raspberries

1. Peel pears, leaving stem intact.
2. Combine sugar and the water in large saucepan; stir over low heat until sugar dissolves. Split vanilla bean in half lengthways; scrape seeds directly into syrup. Add the pears and approximately one-third of the raspberries to the pan; bring to a boil. Simmer, covered, about 20 minutes or until pears are just tender, turning pears occasionally during cooking; cool.
3. Place pears and syrup in large bowl. Cover; refrigerate overnight, turning pears occasionally.
4. One hour before serving, add remaining raspberries; stir gently to combine, then refrigerate.

SERVES 6

per serving 0.2g fat; 896kJ

tip Corella pears are miniature dessert pears; if unavailable, use beurre bosc pears - sweet, juicy pears with greenish-brown to russet-brown skin and very white flesh.

serving suggestion Sprinkle about 1/2 teaspoon of finely chopped fresh mint over each portion and serve with softly whipped cream, if desired. Don't forget to have a selection of chocolates on the table (vanilla and chocolate are made for one another).

brandied apricot *ice-cream*

preparation time 15 minutes ■ cooking time 5 minutes (plus freezing time)

1 cup (150g) dried apricots
1/4 cup (60ml) brandy
300ml cream
1 cup (250ml) milk
4 egg yolks
1/2 cup (110g) sugar

1. Blend or process apricots with brandy until chopped finely.
2. Combine cream and milk in medium saucepan. Cook, stirring, until hot; do not boil.
3. Beat egg yolks and sugar in medium bowl with electric mixer until thick and creamy; gradually beat in cream mixture.
4. Stir apricot mixture into egg mixture.
5. Pour into 1.25 litre (5-cup) pudding steamer. Cover; freeze about 3 hours or until just set.
6. Place ice-cream in large bowl; beat with electric mixer until smooth. Line steamer with plastic wrap; return ice-cream to steamer. Cover; freeze overnight or until set.

SERVES 6

MAKES 4 CUPS (1 LITRE)

per serving 26.8g fat; 1706kJ

tips You may prefer to use an ice-cream maker if you own one.

When you freeze the ice-cream for the final time, you can put it in any container (or even several small containers) of your choice.

flourless chocolate hazelnut *cake*

preparation time 15 minutes ■ cooking time 1 hour 15 minutes

The rich, dense hazelnut meal in this recipe is used instead of flour.

- 1/3 cup (35g) cocoa powder
- 1/3 cup (80ml) hot water
- 150g dark chocolate, melted
- 150g unsalted butter, melted
- 1 1/3 cups (275g) firmly packed brown sugar
- 1 cup (110g) hazelnut meal
- 4 eggs, separated

1. Preheat oven to moderate. Grease deep 20cm-round cake pan; line base and side with baking paper.
2. Combine cocoa and the water in large bowl; stir until smooth. Add chocolate, butter, sugar and hazelnut meal; stir until combined. Stir in egg yolks, one at a time, stirring well after each addition.
3. Beat egg whites in small bowl with electric mixer until soft peaks form; fold, in two batches, into chocolate mixture.
4. Pour mixture into prepared pan. Bake in moderate oven about 1 1/4 hours; cool in pan.

SERVES 8

per serving 32.6g fat; 2086kJ

tip This cake keeps very well under refrigeration, so it can be made up to four days ahead and refrigerated, covered (it's also suitable to freeze for up to three months).

serving suggestion Dust with sifted cocoa powder; serve with separate bowls of mixed berries and thickened cream.

watermelon *granita*

with gingered pineapple

preparation time 30 minutes ■ cooking time 30 minutes
(plus cooling, freezing and refrigeration time)

This recipe has to be made several hours before serving, but if you make it the night before, you'll have less to do when the gang's on the way.

2kg watermelon, chopped coarsely
3/4 cup (165g) sugar
2 cups (500ml) water
50g piece ginger, sliced finely
1/4 cup (60ml) green ginger wine
1/2 cup (110g) sugar, extra
3 cups (750ml) water, extra
1 small pineapple (800g), chopped coarsely
4 egg whites
1 tablespoon finely chopped fresh mint leaves

1. Blend or process watermelon until pureed; push through a sieve into large bowl. Discard seeds and pulp; reserve watermelon juice.
2. Combine sugar and the water in medium saucepan. Stir over low heat until sugar dissolves; bring to a boil. Simmer, uncovered, without stirring, 10 minutes; cool.
3. Pour sugar syrup into bowl with watermelon juice; stir until combined. Pour granita mixture into a 20cm x 30cm lamington pan. Cover with foil; freeze about 3 hours or until granita mixture is just set.
4. Meanwhile, combine ginger, wine, extra sugar and extra water in large saucepan; stir over low heat until sugar dissolves. Bring to a boil; simmer, uncovered, without stirring, 10 minutes. Pour syrup into large heatproof bowl. Add pineapple; cool. Cover; refrigerate 3 hours or overnight.
5. When granita mixture is just set, remove from freezer and place in large bowl with egg whites; beat with electric mixer until smooth. Pour into 14cm x 21cm loaf pan. Cover; freeze overnight or until frozen.
6. Just before serving, stir mint into gingered pineapple; serve with watermelon granita.

SERVES 6

per serving 0.5g fat; 1178kJ

tip You could substitute honeydew melon for watermelon, if you prefer.

serving suggestion Coconut macaroons go beautifully with the flavours in this dessert.

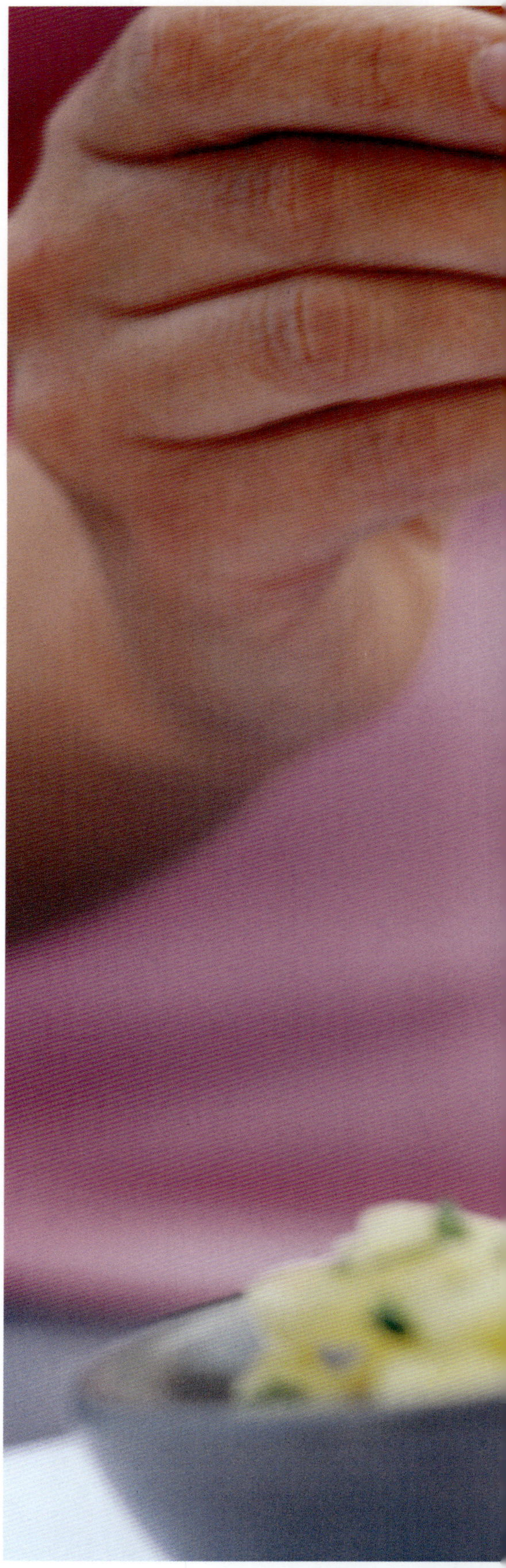

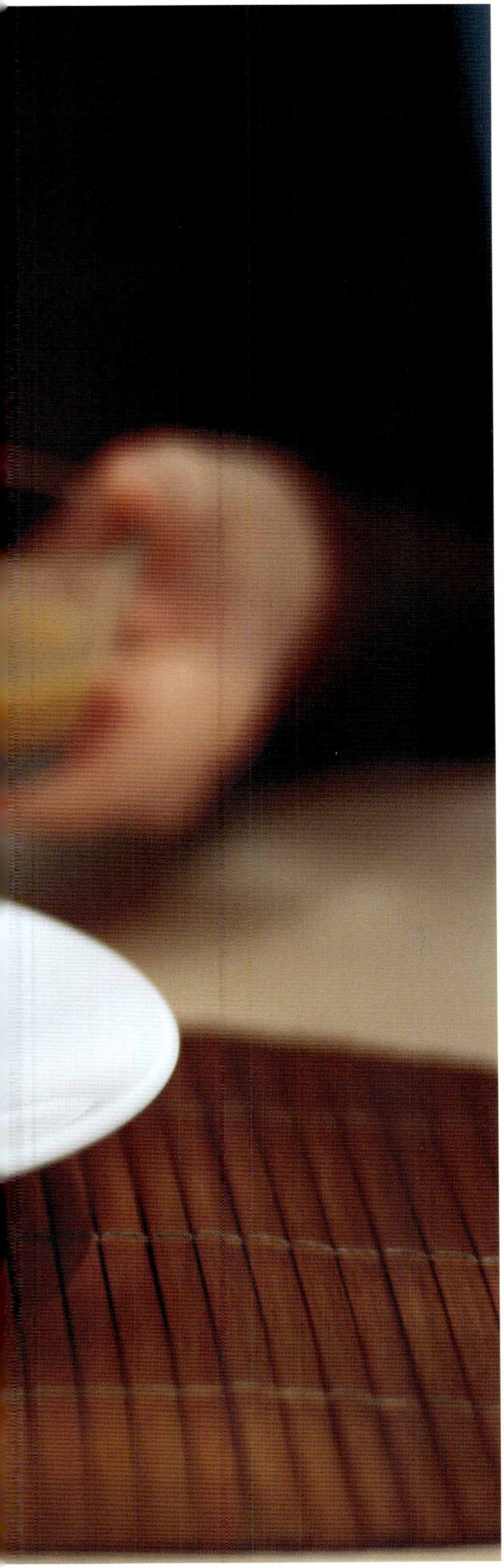

sticky date *pudding*
with butterscotch sauce

preparation time 10 minutes (plus standing time)
cooking time 1 hour (plus standing time)

1¼ cups (200g) seeded dried dates
1¼ cups (310ml) boiling water
1 teaspoon bicarbonate of soda
50g butter, chopped
½ cup (100g) firmly packed brown sugar
2 eggs, beaten lightly
1 cup (150g) self-raising flour

BUTTERSCOTCH SAUCE

¾ cup (150g) firmly packed brown sugar
300ml cream
80g butter

1. Preheat oven to moderate. Grease deep 20cm-round cake pan; line base with baking paper.
2. Combine dates and the water in medium heatproof bowl. Stir in soda; stand 5 minutes.
3. Blend or process date mixture with butter and sugar until pureed. Add eggs and flour; blend or process until just combined. Pour mixture into prepared pan.
4. Bake, uncovered, in moderate oven about 1 hour (cover with foil if pudding starts to overbrown). Stand 10 minutes; turn onto serving plate. Serve warm with butterscotch sauce.

butterscotch sauce Combine ingredients in medium saucepan; stir over low heat until sauce is smooth and slightly thickened.

SERVES 6

per serving 41.3g fat; 2974kJ

tips Both the pudding and sauce can be made a day ahead and refrigerated, covered, separately.

You can freeze the pudding for up to three months. Defrost and warm in microwave oven while making the butterscotch sauce.

serving suggestion This pudding is good served warm with sliced fresh strawberries and thickened cream.

lime macaroon *tart*

preparation time 30 minutes (plus refrigeration time) ■ cooking time 1 hour (plus cooling and refrigeration time)

1 cup (150g) plain flour
1/4 cup (40g) icing sugar mixture
100g butter, chopped
1 egg yolk
1 teaspoon iced water

LIME FILLING

2 teaspoons finely grated lime rind
1/4 cup (60ml) lime juice
4 eggs
1/3 cup (75g) sugar
1 cup (250ml) cream

MACAROON TOPPING

2 egg whites
1/2 cup (110g) sugar
1/2 cup (35g) shredded coconut, toasted

1. Preheat oven to moderately hot. Grease 11cm x 35cm rectangular, or 20cm-round, loose-based flan tin.
2. Blend or process flour, sugar, butter, yolk and the water until ingredients just come together. Knead dough gently on floured surface until smooth. Cover; refrigerate 30 minutes.
3. Roll pastry between sheets of baking paper until large enough to line prepared tin; lift pastry into tin. Ease into sides; trim edges. To prevent pastry from shrinking during baking, place pastry-lined tin in refrigerator, covered, for 30 minutes before baking.
4. Cover pastry with baking paper; fill with dried beans or rice. Place tin on oven tray; bake in moderately hot oven 15 minutes. Remove paper and beans; bake, uncovered, 10 minutes or until pastry is browned. Cool; refrigerate until cold. Reduce oven temperature to moderately slow.
5. Pour lime filling into pastry case. Bake, uncovered, in moderately slow oven about 30 minutes or until filling has set slightly; cool.
6. Spread macaroon topping evenly over tart; cook under hot grill until browned lightly.

lime filling Whisk ingredients in medium bowl. Stand 5 minutes; strain.

macaroon topping Beat egg whites in small bowl with electric mixer until soft peaks form. Gradually add sugar, in batches, beating until dissolved between additions; fold in coconut.

SERVES 6

per serving 40.1g fat; 2604kJ

tip Pastry can be made a day ahead and stored in an airtight container. Lime tart, without topping, is best made a day ahead and refrigerated, covered.

chocolate *mousse*

preparation time 10 minutes ■ cooking time 10 minutes (plus cooling and refrigeration time)

200g dark chocolate
4 eggs, separated
1 tablespoon coffee-flavoured liqueur
300ml thickened cream

1 Melt chocolate in large heatproof bowl over saucepan of simmering water. Remove from heat; cool 10 minutes.

2 Stir in egg yolks and liqueur.

3 Beat cream in small bowl with electric mixer until soft peaks form. Fold cream, in two batches, into chocolate mixture.

4 Beat egg whites in small bowl with electric mixer until stiff peaks form; fold into chocolate mixture.

5 Spoon mousse into eight 2/3-cup (160ml) cups or glasses. Refrigerate, uncovered, about 3 hours or until mousse is set.

SERVES 8

per serving 23.6g fat; 1277kJ

tips Try substituting crème de menthe for the coffee-flavoured liqueur – a new way of serving after-dinner mints!

When melting chocolate, be careful that the bottom of the container holding the chocolate does not touch the hot water; the heat of the water will cause the chocolate to burn.

serving suggestion This mousse is delicious with almond biscotti, a twice-baked Italian biscuit that you can purchase at most supermarkets.

panettone

custards with macadamia toffee

preparation time 20 minutes ■ cooking time 40 minutes (plus standing time)

A traditional Italian sweet yeast cake, panettone is rich in sultanas, pine nuts and candied fruit, and sometimes contains chocolate or one of several fillings. Associated with Christmas giving, this large cake is also a staple at christenings and weddings. This recipe makes good use of leftover panettone.

Boiling sugar syrup so toffee starts to colour

Pouring toffee over nuts on oven tray

Chopping toffee coarsely

500g panettone
50g softened butter
3 1/2 cups (875ml) milk
1 vanilla bean, halved lengthways
4 eggs
1 cup (220g) sugar
3/4 cup (110g) macadamias, chopped coarsely
2 tablespoons water

1. Preheat oven to moderately slow. Grease six 1-cup (250ml) ovenproof dishes.
2. Cut panettone into 1.5cm-thick rounds; spread each round with butter on one side. Cut each round into quarters; divide among prepared dishes.
3. Combine milk and vanilla bean in medium saucepan; bring almost to a boil. Remove from heat; stand, covered, 10 minutes.
4. Meanwhile, whisk eggs and half of the sugar in large heatproof jug. Gradually whisk hot milk mixture into egg mixture. Strain into large jug; discard vanilla bean.
5. Carefully pour egg mixture over panettone in prepared dishes. Place dishes in large baking dish; add enough boiling water to come halfway up sides of dishes. Bake, uncovered, in moderately slow oven about 30 minutes or until set.
6. Meanwhile, place nuts on oven tray; toast, uncovered, in oven with panettone about 10 minutes or until browned lightly. Place remaining sugar and the water in small saucepan; stir over heat, without boiling, until sugar dissolves. Boil, uncovered, without stirring, about 10 minutes or until sugar syrup is golden brown; pour over nuts. Cool; chop toffee coarsely.
7. Serve custards topped with toffee; dust tops lightly with icing sugar, if desired.

SERVES 6

per serving 51.5g fat; 3748kJ

tip Brioche, hot cross buns or fruit loaf can be used instead of panettone.

serving suggestion As this is a rich dessert, it would be best served at the end of a fairly light meal, accompanied by espresso.

almond apple *flan*

preparation time 30 minutes ■ cooking time 40 minutes (plus cooling and refrigeration time)

1¼ cups (185g) plain flour
90g butter, chopped
¼ cup (55g) sugar
2 egg yolks
1 tablespoon water, approximately
2 medium apples (300g)
2 tablespoons apricot jam

Cutting the peeled and cored apples into quarters

ALMOND FILLING
125g butter, softened
⅓ cup (75g) sugar
2 eggs
1 cup (125g) almond meal
1 tablespoon plain flour

Slicing each apple quarter at 3mm intervals

1 Blend or process flour, butter, sugar, egg yolks and enough of the water until ingredients just come together. Knead dough gently on floured surface until smooth. Cover; refrigerate 30 minutes.

2 Preheat oven to moderate. Grease 24cm-round loose-based flan tin. Roll pastry between sheets of baking paper until large enough to line prepared tin. Ease pastry into tin; trim edges. Place pastry-lined tin, covered, in refrigerator 30 minutes before baking.

3 Peel and core apples then cut into quarters. Slice each quarter at 3mm intervals, taking care not to cut all the way through; sliced quarters should remain connected.

Arranging apple quarters on flan filling

4 Spread almond filling into pastry case; arrange apple quarters on top, cut-side up, pressing lightly into filling. Bake in moderate oven about 40 minutes or until browned lightly. Brush hot flan with warmed sieved apricot jam; cool in tin.

almond filling Beat butter and sugar in small bowl with electric mixer until just combined. Add eggs, one at a time, beating well between each addition; fold in almond meal and flour.

SERVES 8

per serving 33.8g fat; 2097kJ

tips Don't peel or slice the apples until you're ready to finish assembling the flan, because they will discolour.

You can use warmed sieved fig and almond preserves, instead of apricot jam, to brush over the hot flan.

Flan can be made a day ahead and stored in an airtight container.

serving suggestion This dessert is fabulous with a scoop of vanilla ice-cream melting on top.

chocolate-meringue *tiramisu*

preparation time 50 minutes ■ cooking time 50 minutes (plus cooling and refrigeration time)

Tiramisu, translated roughly as "pick-me-up", is usually made of savoiardi (lady-fingers) soaked in coffee and marsala, then layered with mascarpone. Our version takes sublime liberties with the original!

6 egg whites
1 cup (220g) caster sugar
$^1/_2$ cup (100g) firmly packed brown sugar
60g dark chocolate, grated

COFFEE FILLING

2 teaspoons instant coffee powder
2 teaspoons hot water
300ml thickened cream
250g mascarpone cheese
$^1/_4$ cup (60ml) coffee-flavoured liqueur

1 Preheat oven to slow. Line two oven trays with baking paper; trace a 22cm circle on each sheet of baking paper.

2 Beat egg whites in large bowl with electric mixer until soft peaks form. Add both sugars, in batches, beating until dissolved between additions (this will take about 15 minutes).

3 Spread equal amounts of egg white mixture between the two circle tracings; bake, uncovered, in slow oven about 50 minutes or until firm, swapping position of trays halfway during cooking. Cool meringues in oven with door ajar.

4 Spread half of the coffee filling over one meringue; sprinkle with half of the chocolate. Top with remaining meringue; spread with remaining filling, then sprinkle with remaining chocolate. Refrigerate, covered, 3 hours or overnight, before serving.

coffee filling Combine coffee and the water in small jug; stir until coffee dissolves. Beat cream in small bowl with electric mixer until soft peaks form; fold in coffee mixture, mascarpone and liqueur.

SERVES 8

per serving 31.3g fat; 2134kJ

tip Make certain both the bowl and your beaters are thoroughly grease-free and dry before beating egg whites.

serving suggestion Serve decorated with chocolate curls and strawberries. To make chocolate curls, spread a thin layer of melted chocolate over a cool surface, such as a large marble or ceramic tile; leave to set at room temperature. Use a large sharp knife, hold it at a 45-degree angle and pull knife gently over the surface of chocolate to form curls.

Spreading meringue mixture in the circle tracing

Layering meringues

oven-roasted cardamom *quinces* with gingered cream

preparation time 10 minutes ■ cooking time 2 hours 10 minutes

Cooking time will vary, depending on how ripe the quinces are.

4 medium quinces (1.3kg), peeled
2½ cups (625ml) water
1 cup (220g) sugar
1 tablespoon lemon juice
6 cardamom pods, bruised
2 cinnamon sticks
300ml rich cream
2 tablespoons finely chopped ginger in syrup

1. Preheat oven to moderate. Lightly grease a large baking dish.
2. Cut each quince into eight wedges. Place quince wedges, in a single layer, in prepared baking dish.
3. Combine the water, sugar, juice, cardamom and cinnamon in medium saucepan. Stir over low heat until sugar dissolves. Bring to a boil; simmer, uncovered, 5 minutes.
4. Pour hot syrup over quince. Cook, in moderate oven, covered, about 2 hours or until quince is rosy pink and tender, turning occasionally.
5. Just before serving, combine cream and ginger in small bowl; serve with oven-roasted quince.

SERVES 8

per serving 20.9g fat; 1633kJ

tips Quinces can be made up to two days ahead. The longer you cook the quinces the pinker they become.

with coffee...

orange syrup *cake*

preparation time 20 minutes
cooking time 50 minutes (plus standing time)

125g butter
1/2 cup (110g) sugar
2 eggs
1 3/4 cups (260g) self-raising flour
1/2 cup (125ml) buttermilk
1 tablespoon finely grated orange rind
1/4 cup (60ml) orange juice

ORANGE SYRUP
1 cup (250ml) orange juice
1/2 cup (110g) sugar

1. Preheat oven to moderate. Grease 14cm x 21cm loaf pan; line base and two long sides with baking paper.
2. Beat butter and sugar in medium bowl with electric mixer until light and fluffy. Add eggs, one at a time, beating until just combined between each addition.
3. Stir in flour, buttermilk, rind and juice, in two batches; spread cake mixture into prepared pan. Bake in moderate oven about 50 minutes; stand 5 minutes. Turn onto wire rack placed over oven tray; pour hot orange syrup over hot cake.
4. To serve, cut cake into 2cm slices.

orange syrup Combine juice and sugar in small saucepan; stir over low heat, without boiling, until sugar dissolves. Bring to a boil; simmer, uncovered, without stirring, about 10 minutes or until syrup thickens slightly.

MAKES 10 SLICES

per slice 12g fat; 1240kJ

tips Make the syrup while the cake is in the oven.

You can replace the orange rind and juice in this recipe with equivalent amounts of lemon or lime, if you prefer.

This cake is suitable to freeze; wrap tightly in plastic wrap and freeze for up to three months.

serving suggestion Serve hot or cold with thickened cream and candied oranges.

mandarin *shortbread* sticks

preparation time 15 minutes ■ cooking time 20 minutes (plus cooling time)

250g butter
1/2 cup (80g) icing sugar mixture
2 tablespoons rice flour
2 cups (300g) plain flour
2 tablespoons finely grated mandarin rind
1/4 cup (60ml) mandarin juice
1/2 cup (75g) macadamias, toasted, chopped finely
60g dark chocolate, melted

1 Preheat oven to moderate.

2 Beat butter and sugar in medium bowl with electric mixer until light and fluffy. Transfer mixture to large bowl; fold in both flours, rind, juice and nuts.

3 Knead mixture, gently, on floured surface until smooth. Roll level tablespoons of mixture into 15cm-long sticks; place sticks 3cm apart on greased oven trays. Bake in moderate oven about 20 minutes or until firm. Cool shortbread sticks on trays for 5 minutes; lift onto wire rack to cool. Drizzle shortbread with melted chocolate.

MAKES 30

per stick 9.4g fat; 577kJ

tips If mixture is overly soft, refrigerate 10 minutes before rolling.

These shortbread sticks can be made one week ahead and stored in an airtight container. Uncooked shortbread can be frozen for up to three months.

Take care when melting chocolate to ensure it does not come into contact with water. If it does, it will "seize", that is, become lumpy and lose its sheen. If this occurs, you will have to start over with a new piece of chocolate. For this reason, never cover chocolate when melting it: the condensation that forms inside the saucepan lid will drop beads of moisture into the chocolate.

meringue kisses with passionfruit cream

preparation time 20 minutes ■ cooking time 30 minutes (plus cooling time)

1 egg white
1/2 teaspoon white vinegar
1/3 cup (75g) sugar
1 teaspoon icing sugar mixture
1/4 cup (60ml) thickened cream
1 tablespoon icing sugar mixture, extra
1 tablespoon passionfruit pulp

1 Preheat oven to very slow. Grease oven trays; dust with cornflour, shaking off excess.

2 Beat egg white, vinegar and sugar in small bowl with electric mixer about 10 minutes or until sugar dissolves; fold in icing sugar.

3 Place meringue mixture into piping bag fitted with small plain nozzle; pipe 1.5cm rounds 3cm apart onto prepared trays. Bake in very slow oven about 30 minutes or until crisp and dry. Cool meringues on trays.

4 Beat cream, 2 teaspoons of the extra icing sugar and passionfruit in small bowl with electric mixer until stiff peaks form.

5 Sandwich meringues together with passionfruit cream; dust with extra remaining icing sugar.

MAKES 35

per kiss 0.6g fat; 72kJ

tip Meringues can be made two days ahead and stored in airtight containers.

serving suggestion Serve with a bowl of fresh raspberries.

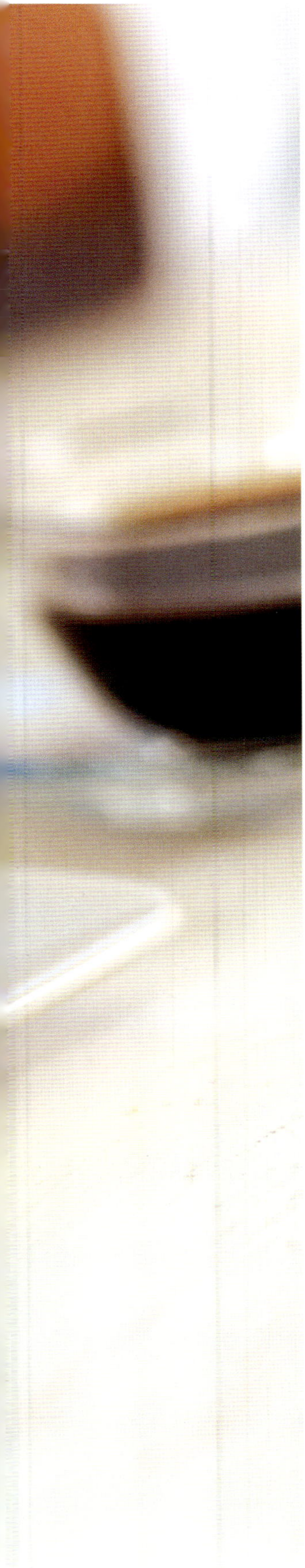

pistachio bread

preparation time 10 minutes ■ cooking time 45 minutes (plus standing time)

3 egg whites
1/3 cup (75g) sugar
1/4 teaspoon ground cardamom
1 teaspoon finely grated orange rind
3/4 cup (110g) plain flour
3/4 cup (110g) shelled pistachios

Spreading mixture into prepared pan before baking

After first baking: cutting bread diagonally into 3mm slices

Second baking of slices on ungreased oven trays

1 Preheat oven to moderate. Grease 8cm x 26cm bar pan; line base and sides with baking paper, extending paper 2cm above long sides of pan.

2 Beat egg whites in small bowl with electric mixer until soft peaks form. With motor operating, gradually add sugar, beating until dissolved between additions. Fold in cardamom, rind, flour and nuts; spread bread mixture into prepared pan.

3 Bake in moderate oven about 30 minutes or until browned lightly; cool in pan. Wrap in foil; stand overnight.

4 Preheat oven to slow.

5 Using a serrated or electric knife, cut bread into 3mm diagonal slices. Place slices on ungreased oven trays. Bake in slow oven about 15 minutes or until dry and crisp; turn onto wire rack to cool.

MAKES 70

per slice 0.8g fat; 79kJ

tips Uncut bread can be frozen after the first baking.

After the second baking, bread slices can be kept up to four days if stored in an airtight container.

For a different spiced version, omit the cardamom and use 1/2 teaspoon ground cinnamon and 1/4 teaspoon ground nutmeg instead.

serving suggestion These small, crisp slices are made for dunking, so serve them with coffee or tea.

white chocolate and frangelico *truffles*

preparation time 35 minutes ■ cooking time 5 minutes (plus refrigeration time)

Frangelico is a hazelnut-flavoured liqueur that marries devastatingly well with chocolate.

1/4 cup (60ml) cream
30g butter
250g white chocolate, chopped finely
1/4 cup (35g) roasted hazelnuts, chopped finely
2 tablespoons Frangelico
200g dark chocolate, melted
100g white chocolate, melted, extra

1 Place cream, butter and white chocolate in medium saucepan; stir over low heat until chocolate melts. Stir in hazelnuts and liqueur; pour mixture into small bowl. Cover; refrigerate, stirring occasionally, about 1 hour or until mixture thickens but does not set.

2 Roll rounded teaspoons of mixture into balls; refrigerate truffles on tray until they become firm.

3 Working rapidly, dip the truffles in the melted dark chocolate then roll gently in hands to coat evenly; return truffles to same tray.

4 Drizzle truffles with melted white chocolate; refrigerate, uncovered, until chocolate is completely set.

MAKES 32

per truffle 7.3g fat; 495kJ

tips It's best to make these truffles a day ahead and store in an airtight container.

Don't melt chocolate in a plastic bowl because plastic is not a good heat conductor. One of the best ways to melt chocolate is in an uncovered microwave-safe container on HIGH (100%) in 30-second bursts, removing it immediately when melted.

Dipping truffles in the melted dark chocolate

Rolling truffles gently in hands to coat evenly with chocolate

Drizzling truffles with melted white chocolate

raspberry mini *friands*

preparation time 15 minutes ■ cooking time 15 minutes (plus cooling time)

These are the little cakes you find in nearly every smart coffee shop; they come in a variety of flavours but we like the raspberry ones best. You can use almond meal (finely ground almonds) instead of the hazelnut meal, if you prefer; either one makes a great friand. You will need 90 mini paper cases for this recipe; two cases are used for each friand to support the mixture.

cooking-oil spray
1/2 cup (55g) hazelnut meal
3/4 cup (120g) icing sugar mixture
1/4 cup (35g) plain flour
90g butter, melted
3 egg whites, beaten lightly
100g raspberries, approximately
1/4 cup (20g) flaked almonds

1. Preheat oven to moderately hot. Place mini paper cases, doubled, on oven tray; spray lightly with cooking-oil spray.
2. Place hazelnut meal, icing sugar and flour in medium bowl. Add butter and egg whites; stir until just combined.
3. Divide mixture among cases; place one raspberry in the centre of each case and scatter almonds on top. Bake in moderately hot oven about 15 minutes; cool friands on wire rack.

MAKES 45

per friand 2.7g fat; 166kJ

tip You can make these friands ahead and freeze until needed. Place in a freezer bag and freeze for up to three months.

serving suggestion These are a real treat in the lunchbox for both small and big "children".

cheese platter

with grilled fresh tamarillos, muscatels and pecan date loaf

preparation time 30 minutes
cooking time 40 minutes (plus cooling time)

Make up a platter of four or five of your favourite cheeses: a 125g wedge of each is sufficient for eight people when served with the other components of this recipe. We suggest you include some or all of the following among your selection: a mild, creamy brie-like blue; a hard-textured cheese with a bit of bite like appenzeller, emmentaler or gruyère; a semi-firm full-flavoured cheese such as port-salut, havarti or provolone; a ripe and runny triple-cream brie; and, last but certainly not least, one of your area's best cheddars. Dried cherries, blueberries and cranberries also provide a nice touch when scattered among the cheeses on the platter.

8 fresh medium tamarillos (800g), halved
1/4 cup (55g) demerara sugar
200g dried muscatel grapes

PECAN DATE LOAF

1 cup (170g) seeded dried dates, chopped coarsely
60g butter
2 tablespoons golden syrup
1 cup (200g) firmly packed brown sugar
3/4 cup (180ml) water
1/2 teaspoon bicarbonate of soda
2 teaspoons ground ginger
1 egg, beaten lightly
1/2 cup (50g) pecans, chopped coarsely
2 cups (300g) self-raising flour

1. Place tamarillos, cut-side up, on oven tray; sprinkle with sugar. Place under hot grill about 10 minutes, or until sugar melts and browns and tamarillos are just tender.
2. Serve tamarillos with cheeses, pecan date loaf and grapes.

pecan date loaf Preheat oven to moderate. Grease two 8cm x 17cm nut roll tins and lids; place one lid on each tin. Combine dates, butter, syrup, sugar and the water in medium saucepan. Stir over low heat until sugar dissolves; bring to a boil. Remove from heat; cool. Stir in soda, ginger, egg, nuts and flour; mix well. Spoon mixture into prepared tins; place remaining lids on tins. Stand on oven tray; bake in moderate oven about 40 minutes. Cool loaves in tins 10 minutes; turn onto wire rack to cool.

SERVES 8

per serving 12.2g fat; 2222kJ (without cheese)

tips Lightly oil your tablespoon so measuring golden syrup is easier.

This pecan loaf is suitable for freezing up to three months, wrapped tightly in plastic wrap.

If you don't have nut roll tins, you can use an 8cm x 26cm bar cake pan instead.

menu ideas

VEGETARIAN DINNER

mediterranean grilled vegetables with tomato vinaigrette p.25

ricotta and capsicum ravioli with rocket dressing p.56

chocolate-meringue tiramisu p.102

pistachio bread p.109

A FORTNIGHT AHEAD make pistachio bread to first baking; freeze.

FOUR DAYS AHEAD slice pistachio bread and bake. Store slices in airtight container.

A DAY AHEAD make tomato vinaigrette; prepare ravioli. Make chocolate-meringue tiramisu.

THREE HOURS AHEAD make rocket dressing; cover dressing surface with plastic wrap to prevent oxidation.

ONE HOUR AHEAD grill vegetables.

JAPANESE DINNER

tuna and avocado rice paper rolls p.30

vegetables and udon in chicken-miso broth p.47

watermelon granita with gingered pineapple p.92

THREE DAYS AHEAD make watermelon granita and freeze.

A DAY AHEAD prepare chicken stock for broth; macerate pineapple in ginger syrup.

THREE HOURS AHEAD make tuna and avocado rice paper rolls.

LATE SUMMER LUNCH

pizza with prosciutto and ricotta p.41

chicken parmesan with basil sauce p.49

vine-ripened tomatoes and goat cheese in walnut dressing p.74

zucchini ribbon salad with spearmint and almonds p.81

poached pears in raspberry and vanilla-bean syrup p.89

white chocolate and frangelico truffles p.110

SEVERAL WEEKS AHEAD crumb chicken; freeze until required.

A DAY AHEAD toast nuts for salads. Poach pears in raspberry syrup. Make truffles.

AN HOUR AHEAD assemble pizzas; add remaining raspberries to syrup.

SEAFOOD DINNER

marinated octopus salad p.43

prawn and asparagus risotto p.67

mesclun with pine nuts in lime vinaigrette p.77

brandied apricot ice-cream p.90

THREE DAYS AHEAD make ice-cream.

A DAY AHEAD cook octopus; marinate overnight. Make chicken stock for risotto. Make lime vinaigrette.

THREE HOURS AHEAD add vegetables to octopus salad.

CHINESE DINNER

prawn wontons with sweet chilli sauce p.14

lemon chicken with fresh egg noodles p.65

asian greens in oyster sauce p.78

A DAY AHEAD make prawn wontons up to cooking stage (can be frozen for up to three months).

ONE HOUR AHEAD prepare vegetables and chicken.

AUTUMN LUNCH

tandoori lamb cutlets with cucumber salad p.34

lentil salad with sesame seeds and coriander p.76

cheese platter with grilled fresh tamarillos, muscatels and pecan date loaf p.112

meringue kisses with passionfruit cream p.107

TWO DAYS AHEAD prepare tandoori paste for lamb.

A DAY AHEAD make pecan date loaf; cook meringues and store in an airtight container with baking paper between layers. Cook lentils for salad. Marinate lamb cutlets.

AN HOUR AHEAD make passionfruit cream; sandwich meringue kisses. Assemble cheese platter.

MOROCCAN DINNER

carrot and roasted red capsicum soup p.37

seared salmon with pistachio-coriander pesto and pumpkin couscous p.62

oven-roasted cardamom quinces with gingered cream p.103

UP TO TWO DAYS AHEAD make pesto for salmon. Roast the quinces.

A DAY AHEAD make soup.

ASIAN FINGER FOOD

sushi selection p.20-23

chicken wing trio p.16

peking duck crepes p.19

vegetable tempura with wasabi aioli p.28

A DAY AHEAD prepare wasabi aioli; marinate chicken wings (can also be marinated and frozen up to two months in advance).

THREE HOURS AHEAD make crepes and prepare duck; make sushi.

ELEGANT SUPPER

oysters with smoked salmon p.27

chorizo, potato and basil frittata p.7

broad bean salad with anchovy dressing p.83

flourless chocolate hazelnut cake p.91

UP TO THREE DAYS AHEAD make flourless chocolate hazelnut cake.

A DAY AHEAD make frittata; prepare ricotta topping for oysters. Make dressing for broad bean salad.

FIVE HOURS AHEAD thaw and peel broad beans.

WINTER DINNER

warm cherry- and teardrop-tomato salad p.77

grilled scotch fillet steaks with caramelised onion and garlic mushrooms p.66

creamed spinach p.82

kumara mash p.82

sticky date pudding with butterscotch sauce p.95

A DAY AHEAD make sticky date pudding and butterscotch sauce.

AN HOUR AHEAD cook creamed spinach; reheat just before serving.

INDIAN DINNER

kumara and pea samosas with cucumber yogurt p.12

chicken dhania masala p.55

mixed vegetable and lentil curry p.60

lime macaroon tart p.96

A DAY AHEAD make samosas and masala for chicken dish. Make vegetable and lentil curry. Prepare lime tart to filling stage.

THREE HOURS AHEAD fill lime tart and cook under grill.

DO-AHEAD LUNCH

mediterranean vegetable loaf p.44

pappardelle with chilli and semi-dried tomato sauce p.48

orange syrup cake p.104

A DAY AHEAD make pasta sauce. Prepare and assemble mediterranean vegetable loaf. Prepare orange syrup cake.

DO-AHEAD DINNER

beetroot dip and fetta dip p.15

moroccan lamb shanks with polenta and white beans p.59

almond apple flan p.101

TWO DAYS AHEAD make dips, cover tightly with plastic wrap.

A DAY AHEAD make lamb shanks; cook almond apple flan.

THREE HOURS AHEAD prepare crudités.

glossary

bacon rashers also known as slices of bacon; made from pork side, cured, smoked and sliced.

beetroot also known as red beets or simply beets; firm, round root vegetable which can be eaten raw, grated, in salads, or boiled or microwaved then mashed.

bicarbonate of soda also known as baking soda.

broad beans also known as fava beans, these are available fresh, canned and frozen; best eaten when peeled twice (discarding both the long pod and pale-green tough inner shell).

broccolini milder and sweeter than traditional broccoli; completely edible from flower to stem with a delicate flavour with a subtle, peppery edge.

burghul also known as bulghur; dried steamed wheat kernels crushed into small grains. Used in Middle-Eastern cooking.

butter use salted or sweet (unsalted) butter; 125g is equal to 1 stick butter.

capsicum also known as bell pepper or, simply, pepper. Seeds and membranes should be discarded before use.

cheese

BOCCONCINI small rounds of fresh "baby" mozzarella; a delicate, soft white cheese.

FETTA Greek in origin; a crumbly sheep-milk cheese with a sharp, salty taste.

HALOUMI firm cream-coloured sheep-milk cheese matured in brine; best when grilled or fried briefly.

MASCARPONE a thick, triple-cream fresh cheese with a delicately sweet taste.

ROMANO a good-grating hard cheese with a grainy texture and sharp flavour.

chickpeas also called garbanzos, hummus or channa; a sandy-coloured legume used in Mediterranean and Indian cooking.

chillies

BANANA a sweet-flavoured chilli with a long, tapering shape. If unavailable, substitute with capsicum.

DUTCH medium-hot, but flavoursome, fairly long fresh chilli; sometimes referred to as a holland chilli.

JALAPEÑO sold finely chopped or whole, bottled in vinegar, as well as fresh; we used the medium-hot, sweetish chopped bottled version in our recipes.

SWEET CHILLI SAUCE comparatively mild, Thai-type sauce made from red chillies, sugar, garlic and white wine vinegar.

THAI red to dark-green in colour, they are small, medium-to-hot chillies.

chinese green vegetables as these can be called by many different names, we show a few of the alternative names for each vegetable.

BOK CHOY (bak choy, pak choi, chinese white cabbage, chinese chard) fresh, mild mustard taste; use stems and leaves, stir-fry or braise.

TAT SOI (rosette bok choy, tai gu choy, chinese flat cabbage) a variety of bok choy, developed to grow close to the ground so it is easily protected from frost.

chorizo a highly seasoned sausage of Spanish origin, made of ground pork.

ciabatta in Italian, the word means slipper, which is the traditional shape of this popular crusty bread.

coriander also known as cilantro or chinese parsley; bright-green leafy herb with a pungent flavour.

cornflour also known as cornstarch; used as a thickening agent in cooking.

cornmeal ground dried corn (maize); similar to polenta but slightly coarser. Also the name of the dish made from it, and sometimes called cornmeal mush.

couscous a fine, grain-like cereal product originally from North Africa; made from semolina.

cucumber, lebanese long, slender and thin-skinned; this variety is also known as the european or burpless cucumber.

daikon

PICKLED Japanese radish sold pickled in vinegar and citric acid; eaten with raw fish dishes and in salads.

RADISH a large Asian radish with a sweet, fresh taste. In Japan, it is grated and eaten raw as an accompaniment.

RADISH SPROUTS the young shoots of the daikon are often used as a garnish and to add a mild bite to salads.

eggplant also known as aubergine.

eggs some recipes in this book call for raw or barely cooked eggs; exercise care if there are salmonella problems in your area.

fennel also known as finocchio or anise; also the name given to the dried seeds that imparts a licorice flavour to cooked foods.

flour

PLAIN an all-purpose flour, made from wheat.

SELF-RAISING plain flour sifted with baking powder in the ratio of 1 cup flour to 2 teaspoons baking powder.

RICE a very fine flour, made from ground white rice.

food mill also called a mouli; a rotary sieve used for liquidising and pureeing.

gravy beef boneless stewing beef used for slow-cooking soups and casseroles.

hazelnut meal also called ground hazelnuts; nuts are powdered to a flour-like texture, for use in baking or as a thickening agent.

kumara Polynesian name of an orange-fleshed sweet potato confused with yam.

lamb, french-trimmed shanks (also "drumsticks") or cutlets trimmed of all sinew and fat at the narrow end.

mesclun a gourmet salad mix of assorted greens such as young lettuces, mizuna, baby spinach and curly endive.

mince meat also known as ground meat.

mizuna a Japanese green salad leaf with a delicate mustard flavour; often used in mesclun.

muscatel grapes also known as muscat grapes; used to make the sweet dessert wine having the same name. This grape variety is also superb eaten dried, its distinctively musty flavour is good with cheese, chocolate, pork and game.

niçoise olives tiny ovate brown-black olives with a rich nutty flavour; grown in the rough, hilly terrain of Provence, France. Substitute any small brown olive.

nori sheets of paper-thin dried black seaweed used in Japanese cooking as a flavouring, garnish or for wrapping sushi.

onion

GREEN also known as scallion or (incorrectly) shallot; an immature onion picked before the bulb has formed, having a long, bright-green edible stalk.

RED also known as spanish, red spanish or bermuda onion; a sweet-flavoured, large, purple-red onion that is particularly good eaten raw in salads.

SPRING have crisp, narrow, green-leafed tops and a smallish, round, sweet white bulb.

pears
BEURRE BOSC sweet, juicy dessert pear with a long tapering neck and greenish-brown skin which changes to cinnamon-brown when ripe. Ideal cooking pear, particularly for methods such as poaching or baking.
CORELLA miniature dessert pear with colourful green skin with a gold and red blush; the juicy, delicious flavour makes it a popular eating pear to accompany cheese platters.
NASHI also called japanese or asian pear; a member of the pear family but similar in appearance to an apple.

polenta a flour-like cereal made of ground corn (maize); similar to cornmeal but finer and lighter in colour; also the name of the dish made from it.

prawns crustacean also known as shrimp.

pumpkin also known as squash; we used butternut pumpkin in these recipes unless specified otherwise.

rice
ARBORIO large, round-grain rice, well suited to absorb a large amount of cooking liquid; used in risottos.
BASMATI a white, fragrant long-grain rice used in Indian cooking.
CALROSE medium-grain rice; can be used as a substitute for both long- and short-grain varieties.
JASMINE fragrant long-grain rice; substitute white long-grain rice.
KOSHIHIKARI small, round-grain white rice; substitute white short-grain rice.
LONG-GRAIN elongated grains, stay separate when cooked.
PAPER also known as banh trang. Made from rice paste and stamped into rounds. Dipped in water, they become pliable wrappers for fried food and for eating fresh (uncooked) vegetables.

rocket also known as arugula, rugula and rucola; a peppery-tasting green leaf which can be used similarly to baby spinach.

scotch fillet steak also known as beef rib-eye steaks.

snow peas also called mange tout ("eat all"). Snow pea tendrils, the growing shoots of the plant, are sold by greengrocers.

spinach correct name for this leafy green vegetable; often called english spinach or, incorrectly, silverbeet.

stock 1 cup (250ml) stock is the equivalent of 1 cup (250ml) water plus 1 crumbled stock cube (or 1 teaspoon stock powder). If you prefer to make your own fresh stock, see recipes right.

sugar snap peas small pods with small, formed peas inside; they are eaten whole, cooked or uncooked.

vietnamese mint not a mint at all, this narrow-leafed, pungent herb, also known as cambodian mint and laksa leaf (daun laksa), is widely used in many Asian soups and salads.

yogurt we use unflavoured full-fat yogurt in our recipes unless stated otherwise.

zucchini also known as courgette.

make your own stock

These recipes can be made up to four days ahead and refrigerated, covered. Be sure to remove any fat from the surface after the cooled stock has been refrigerated overnight. If the stock is to be kept longer, it is best to freeze it in smaller quantities. All stock recipes make about 2.5 litres (10 cups).

Stock is also available in cans or tetra packs. Stock cubes or powder can be used. As a guide, 1 teaspoon of stock powder or 1 small crumbled stock cube mixed with 1-cup (250ml) water will give a fairly strong stock. Be aware of the salt and fat content of stock cubes and powders, and prepared stocks.

BEEF STOCK

2kg meaty beef bones
2 medium onions (300g)
2 untrimmed sticks celery (300g), chopped
2 medium carrots (250g), chopped
3 bay leaves
2 teaspoons black peppercorns
5 litres (20 cups) water
3 litres (12 cups) water, extra

Place bones and unpeeled chopped onions in baking dish. Bake in hot oven about 1-hour or until bones and onion are well browned. Transfer bones and onion to large saucepan; add celery, carrot, bay leaves, peppercorns and the water. Simmer, uncovered, 3 hours; add the extra water. Simmer, uncovered, further 1 hour; strain.

CHICKEN STOCK

2kg chicken bones
2 medium onions (300g), chopped
2 untrimmed sticks celery (300g), chopped
2 medium carrots (250g), chopped
3 bay leaves
2 teaspoons black peppercorns
5 litres (20 cups) water

Combine ingredients in large saucepan. Simmer, uncovered, 2 hours; strain.

FISH STOCK

1.5kg fish bones
3 litres (12 cups) water
1 medium onion (150g), chopped
2 untrimmed sticks celery (300g), chopped
2 bay leaves
1 teaspoon black peppercorns

Combine ingredients in large saucepan. Simmer, uncovered, 20 minutes; strain.

VEGETABLE STOCK

2 large carrots (360g), chopped
2 large parsnips (360g), chopped
4 medium onions (600g), chopped
12 untrimmed sticks celery (1.8kg), chopped
4 bay leaves
2 teaspoons black peppercorns
6 litres (24 cups) water

Combine ingredients in large saucepan. Simmer, uncovered, 1½ hours; strain.

index

conversion chart

MEASURES

One Australian metric measuring cup holds approximately 250ml; one Australian metric tablespoon holds 20ml; one Australian metric teaspoon holds 5ml.

The difference between one country's measuring cups and another's is within a two- or three-teaspoon variance, and will not affect your cooking results. North America, New Zealand and the United Kingdom use a 15ml tablespoon.

All cup and spoon measurements are level. The most accurate way of measuring dry ingredients is to weigh them. When measuring liquids, use a clear glass or plastic jug with the metric markings.

We use large eggs with an average weight of 60g.

DRY MEASURES

METRIC	IMPERIAL
15g	½oz
30g	1oz
60g	2oz
90g	3oz
125g	4oz (¼lb)
155g	5oz
185g	6oz
220g	7oz
250g	8oz (½lb)
280g	9oz
315g	10oz
345g	11oz
375g	12oz (¾lb)
410g	13oz
440g	14oz
470g	15oz
500g	16oz (1lb)
750g	24oz (1½lb)
1kg	32oz (2lb)

LIQUID MEASURES

METRIC	IMPERIAL
30ml	1 fluid oz
60ml	2 fluid oz
100ml	3 fluid oz
125ml	4 fluid oz
150ml	5 fluid oz (¼ pint/1 gill)
190ml	6 fluid oz
250ml	8 fluid oz
300ml	10 fluid oz (½ pint)
500ml	16 fluid oz
600ml	20 fluid oz (1 pint)
1000ml (1 litre)	1¾ pints

LENGTH MEASURES

METRIC	IMPERIAL
3mm	⅛in
6mm	¼in
1cm	½in
2cm	¾in
2.5cm	1in
5cm	2in
6cm	2½in
8cm	3in
10cm	4in
13cm	5in
15cm	6in
18cm	7in
20cm	8in
23cm	9in
25cm	10in
28cm	11in
30cm	12in (1ft)

OVEN TEMPERATURES

These oven temperatures are only a guide for conventional ovens. For fan-forced ovens, check the manufacturer's manual.

	°C (CELSIUS)	°F (FAHRENHEIT)	GAS MARK
Very slow	120	250	½
Slow	150	275-300	1-2
Moderately slow	160	325	3
Moderate	180	350-375	4-5
Moderately hot	200	400	6
Hot	220	425-450	7-8
Very hot	240	475	9

ARE YOU MISSING SOME COOKBOOKS?

The Australian Women's Weekly Cookbooks are available from bookshops, cookshops, supermarkets and other stores all over the world. You can also buy direct from the publisher, using the order form below.

TITLE	RRP	QTY	TITLE	RRP	QTY
100 Fast Fillets	£6.99		Indian Cooking Class	£6.99	
After Work Fast	£6.99		Japanese Cooking Class	£6.99	
A Taste of Chocolate	£6.99		Just For One	£6.99	
Beginners Cooking Class	£6.99		Just For Two	£6.99	
Beginners Thai	£6.99		Kids' Birthday Cakes	£6.99	
Best Food Fast	£6.99		Kids Cooking	£6.99	
Breads & Muffins	£6.99		Kids' Cooking Step-by-Step	£6.99	
Brunches, Lunches & Treats	£6.99		Low-carb, Low-fat	£6.99	
Cafe Classics	£6.99		Low-fat Food for Life	£6.99	
Cafe Favourites	£6.99		Low-fat Meals in Minutes	£6.99	
Cakes, Bakes & Desserts	£6.99		Main Course Salads	£6.99	
Cakes Biscuits & Slices	£6.99		Mexican	£6.99	
Cakes Cooking Class	£6.99		Middle Eastern Cooking Class	£6.99	
Caribbean Cooking	£6.99		Mince in Minutes	£6.99	
Casseroles	£6.99		Moroccan & the Foods of North Africa	£6.99	
Casseroles & Slow-Cooked Classics	£6.99		Muffins, Scones & Breads	£6.99	
Cheap Eats	£6.99		New Casseroles	£6.99	
Cheesecakes: baked and chilled	£6.99		New Curries	£6.99	
Chicken	£6.99		New Finger Food	£6.99	
Chicken Meals in Minutes	£6.99		New French Food	£6.99	
Chinese & the foods of Thailand,			New Salads	£6.99	
Vietnam, Malaysia & Japan)	£6.99		Party Food and Drink	£6.99	
Chinese Cooking Class	£6.99		Pasta Meals in Minutes	£6.99	
Christmas Cooking	£6.99		Potatoes	£6.99	
Chocs & Treats	£6.99		Quick & Simple Cooking (Apr 08)	£6.99	
Cocktails	£6.99		Rice & Risotto	£6.99	
Cookies & Biscuits	£6.99		Sauces Salsas & Dressings	£6.99	
Cupcakes & Fairycakes	£6.99		Sensational Stir-Fries	£6.99	
Detox	£6.99		Simple Healthy Meals	£6.99	
Dinner Lamb	£6.99		Simple Starters, Mains & Puds	£6.99	
Easy Comfort Food (Apr 08)	£6.99		Soup	£6.99	
Easy Curry	£6.99		Stir-fry	£6.99	
Easy Midweek Meals	£6.99		Superfoods for Exam Success	£6.99	
Easy Spanish-Style	£6.99		Tapas Mezze Antipasto & other bites	£6.99	
Food for Fit and Healthy Kids	£6.99		Thai Cooking Class	£6.99	
Foods of the Mediterranean	£6.99		Traditional Italian	£6.99	
Foods That Fight Back	£6.99		Vegetarian Meals in Minutes	£6.99	
Fresh Food Fast	£6.99		Vegie Food	£6.99	
Fresh Food for Babies & Toddlers	£6.99		Wicked Sweet Indulgences	£6.99	
Good Food for Babies & Toddlers	£6.99		Wok, Meals in Minutes	£6.99	
Greek Cooking Class	£6.99				
Grills	£6.99				
Healthy Heart Cookbook	£6.99		TOTAL COST:	£	

Mr/Mrs/Ms ______________________________

Address ______________________________ Postcode __________

Day time phone ______________________ email* (optional) __________

I enclose my cheque/money order for £ ______________________

or please charge £ ______________________________

to my: ☐ Access ☐ Mastercard ☐ Visa ☐ Diners Club

Card number | | | | | | | | | | | | | | | |

Expiry date __________ 3 digit security code *(found on reverse of card)* __________

Cardholder's name ______________________ Signature __________

To order: Mail or fax – photocopy or complete the order form above, and send your credit card details or cheque payable to: Australian Consolidated Press (UK), ACP Books, 10 Scirocco Close, Moulton Park Office Village, Northampton NN3 6AP. phone (+44) (0)1604 642200 fax (+44) (0)1604 642300 email books@acpuk.com or order online at www.acpuk.com
Non-UK residents: We accept the credit cards listed on the coupon, or cheques, drafts or International Money Orders payable in sterling and drawn on a UK bank. Credit card charges are at the exchange rate current at the time of payment. **Postage and packing UK:** Add £1.00 per order plus £1.75 per book. **Postage and packing overseas:** Add £2.00 per order plus £3.50 per book. All pricing current at time of going to press and subject to change/availability. **Offer ends 31.12.2008**

* By including your email address, you consent to receipt of any email regarding this magazine, and other emails which inform you of ACP's other publications, products, services and events, and to promote third party goods and services you may be interested in.

TEST KITCHEN
Food director Pamela Clark
Associate food editor Alexandra Somerville
Test Kitchen manager Kellie-Marie Thomas
Nutritional information Belinda Farlow

ACP BOOKS
General manager Christine Whiston
Editorial director Susan Tomnay
Creative director Hieu Chi Nguyen
Designers Mary Keep, Caryl Wiggins, Alison Windmill
Director of sales Brian Cearnes
Marketing manager Bridget Cody
Business analyst Ashley Davies
Operations manager David Scotto
International rights enquires Laura Bamford
bamford@acpuk.com

acp books

ACP Books are published by ACP Magazines
a division of PBL Media Pty Limited
Group publisher, Women's lifestyle
Pat Ingram
Director of sales, Women's lifestyle
Lynette Phillips
Commercial manager, Women's lifestyle
Seymour Cohen
Marketing director, Women's lifestyle
Matthew Dominello
Public relations manager, Women's lifestyle
Hannah Deveraux
Creative director, Events, Women's lifestyle
Luke Bonnano
Research Director, Women's lifestyle
Justin Stone
ACP Magazines, Chief Executive officer
Scott Lorson
PBL Media, Chief Executive officer
Ian Law

Produced by ACP Books, Sydney.
Published by ACP Books, a division of ACP Magazines Ltd, 54 Park St, Sydney; GPO Box 4088, Sydney, NSW 2001.
phone (02) 9282 8618 fax (02) 9267 9438.
acpbooks@acpmagazines.com.au
www.acpbooks.com.au
Printed by Dai Nippon in Korea.

Australia Distributed by Network Services, phone +61 2 9282 8777 fax +61 2 9264 3278
networkweb@networkservicescompany.com.au
United Kingdom Distributed by Australian Consolidated Press (UK), phone (01604) 642 200 fax (01604) 642 300
books@acpuk.com
New Zealand Distributed by Netlink Distribution Company, phone (9) 366 9966 ask@ndc.co.nz
South Africa Distributed by PSD Promotions, phone (27 11) 392 6065/6/7
fax (27 11) 392 6079/80
orders@psdprom.co.za

Brunches, lunches and treats: The Australian women's weekly
Includes index.
ISBN 978 1 86396 723 5 (pbk).
1. Brunches. 2. Luncheons. 3. Desserts.
I. Clark, Pamela. II Title: Australian Women's Weekly
641.53

To order books,
phone 136 116 (within Australia).
Send recipe enquiries to:
recipeenquiries@acpmagazines.com.au